ENCYCLOPEDIA OF MAMMALS

VOLUME 9
Lio–Mol

MARSHALL CAVENDISH
NEW YORK • LONDON • TORONTO • SYDNEY

LIONS

RELATIONS

Lions belong to the mammal order Carnivora and the cat family, Felidae. Other members of the family include:

TIGERS

LEOPARDS

JAGUAR

SNOW LEOPARD

CLOUDED LEOPARD

PUMAS

WILDCATS

R. L. Matthews/Planet Earth Pictures

Lions belong to the cat family, within the group of meat-eating mammals called carnivores. The cats are related to civets, hyenas, and mongooses and belong to the superfamily Feloidea. There are thirty-seven species of cats, divided into four genera. The lion is one of four species known as the "great cats."

ORDER
Carnivora
(carnivores)

SUBORDER
Fissipedia
(land-living carnivores)

SUPERFAMILY
Feloidea
(catlike forms)

FAMILY
Felidae
(all cats)

SUBFAMILY
Pantherinae

GENUS
Panthera

SPECIES
leo

KING OF THE BEASTS

SINCE THE BEGINNING OF RECORDED TIME, THE LION HAS BEEN A SYMBOL OF STRENGTH AND MAJESTY. HAILED AS THE "KING OF THE BEASTS," THIS GREAT CAT IS THE TOP PREDATOR OF THE AFRICAN PLAINS

The lion has made a profound impact on human imagination. Its name has become part of our everyday speech; expressions such as "entering the lion's den," "the lion's share," "lion-hearted," and "lionized" are used all the time.

This majestic and awe-inspiring animal is the second largest of the world's big cats. Along with its closest relatives in this group, the tiger (the largest big cat), the jaguar, and the leopard, the lion is often referred to as a "great cat." However, of all the cats—small, big, and great alike—it is probably the lion that has been most thoroughly studied by zoologists.

THE LION'S LINEAGE
Like all cats, the lion is descended from the medium-sized *Pseudaelurus*, which lived in Europe about 20 million years ago. By 16 million years ago, its descendents had reached North America.

The modern genera of cats first appeared about

10 million years ago in Eurasia; by two million years ago big cats, with a combination of lionlike and tiger-like features, were living in East Africa. This is where what were thought to be the first lions appeared—their fossils have been found in the famous Olduvai Gorge in Tanzania. These remains, of creatures that were much larger than the present-day lion, have been dated at between 500,000 and 700,000 years old. Recent research, though, suggests that these early giants may have been more closely related to other great cats than to the lion.

But whatever its exact origins, it is known that by about a quarter of a million years ago, the lion occurred in Eurasia. Lion fossils of this date have been found in Germany, Greece, and Siberia; the animals concerned were huge creatures, probably the largest cats the world has ever seen.

ROARING RELATIVES

The great cats all belong to the genus *Panthera*, and one of the features that distinguishes them from other cats is that they cannot purr—they roar instead. They are able to do so because one of the hyoid bones that support the voice box, or larynx, is replaced by a long elastic ligament. This ligament measures 6 in (15 cm) long and stretches to as much as 8–9 in (20–23 cm) long, creating a wide air

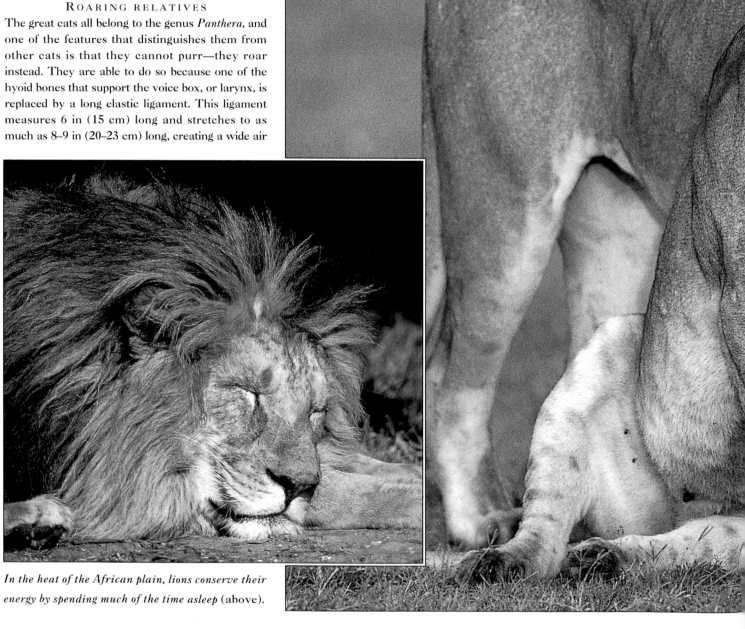

ZEFA

In the heat of the African plain, lions conserve their energy by spending much of the time asleep (above).

Jonathan Scott/Planet Earth Pictures

passage. The vibrations this produces make the lion the noisiest of all its relatives. Its distinctively loud roar is a sound that sends shivers up one's spine when heard in the dead of night in the great African savannas.

A POWERFUL PREDATOR

It is not just the lion's roar that makes it such an awesome creature. Although no longer built on the same scale as its ancestors, the lion still cuts quite a figure when slowly strolling across the savanna. It looks the very symbol of strength and grace; the play of the tremendously powerful muscles under its sleek, tawny coat indicates that it is capable of prodigious feats of strength.

Most of the time, the lion walks slowly, holding its head in line with its back. Its belly swings from side to side, especially when it has recently filled it to capacity with meat from a large kill. But when the need arises, the lion switches to a trot, which is considerably faster than its walk and can be kept up for a long time.

Sometimes, particularly when moving through tall grass, a lion will leap in high, doglike bounds. By contrast, when stalking nervous prey, it flattens itself to a remarkable degree, inching along close to the ground until it is near enough to make the final deadly rush.

In contrast to leopards, which are excellent climbers, lions do not usually spend much time in

---

LION CUBS OFTEN PLAY IN TREES; THEY WILL ALSO TAKE TO THE BRANCHES WHEN CHASED BY PREDATORS

---

trees and have no need of storing their kills there. However, they are perfectly able to climb, and in some areas they regularly take to the trees to rest on stout branches, perhaps to escape the attentions of biting flies.

KEEN SENSES

Lions have excellent eyesight, especially when it comes to distinguishing moving objects. They spend a lot of time watching zebras, wildebeests, and other game animals with a concentrated gaze of their amber eyes. When stalking their prey in open country, they keep their eyes firmly fixed on their quarry. They are able to spot a distant vulture and, knowing that these legendary scavengers are second to none when it comes to finding dead animals, follow its flight path to locate a carcass.

Adult male lions are considerably larger and heavier than adult female lions.

LION
Panthera leo
(pan-THARE-ah LEE-o)

Unlike most other cats, the lion habitually lives in groups, or prides, and hunts cooperatively. By banding together in this way, they are able to overpower and kill prey several times their own size. Recent research suggests that all the African subspecies are so similar that they should be lumped together as a single subspecies distinct from the Asian (or Indian) subspecies.

SUBSPECIES OR RACES
ANGOLAN LION
ASIATIC LION
MASAI LION
SENEGALESE LION
TRANSVAAL LION
BARBARY LION
CAPE LION

Like other cats, lions have relatively big eyes that face forward. This arrangement gives them good binocular vision and depth perception, enabling them to judge distances accurately. Their eyes are superbly adapted to working very efficiently at remarkably low levels of light.

The lion's sense of hearing is also extremely acute, enabling it to hear the smallest sounds made by its prey, the distant calls of jackals or hyenas that might indicate there is a kill to be scavenged, or the far-off grunts of another lion—all sounds that would be inaudible to the human ear.

Although, like other cats, lions have a keen sense of smell, it is not as well developed as in dogs or other carnivores. This sense seems to be far less important to lions in hunting than vision and hearing. But smell is of great importance in their social life, enabling the great cats to learn a great deal about one another from the scents they leave behind them. ■

PUMA

CHEETAH

WILDCAT GROUP
(OLD WORLD)

ANCESTORS OF
PANTHERINE CATS
EVOLVED ABOUT THREE
MILLION YEARS AGO

EXTINCT BY 9,400
YEARS AGO
SABER-TOOTHS

PALLAS'S CAT

ANCESTORS
OF WILDCATS
EVOLVED ABOUT
TEN MILLION
YEARS AGO

Color illustrations Kim Thompson

THE LION'S FAMILY TREE

Today there are eight species in the cat family known as the big cats.
Of these, four—the lion, tiger, leopard, and jaguar—are often referred to as
the great cats, a group that is thought to have diverged from the other cats
between two and three million years ago. It is likely that the leopard and
jaguar evolved more recently than the lion and tiger and thus are more closely
related to one another than to the two other great cats.

JAGUAR

TIGER

LEOPARD

SNOW LEOPARD

OCELOT

ANCESTORS OF OCELOTS
EVOLVED IN CENTRAL ASIA
ABOUT TWELVE MILLION
YEARS AGO, THEN MOVED
TO NORTH AMERICA ABOUT
SIX TO SEVEN MILLION
YEARS LATER

LYNX

MARBLED CAT

B/W illustrations Ruth Grewcock

PSEUDAELURUS
(FIRST-TIME CAT)
SIXTEEN TO TWENTY
MILLION YEARS AGO

ANATOMY:
THE LION

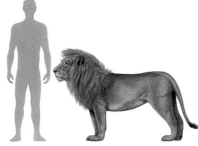

The lion is the second largest of the cats (the tiger is the largest) and one of the world's biggest land carnivores. Males can exceed 9.8 ft (3 m) in head-to-tail length and stand as high as 3 ft (1 m) at the shoulder. The black-footed cat of southern Africa is only 2.3 ft (70 cm) long and, at 2–4 lb (1–2 kg), averages only one-hundredth the weight of its mighty relative.

SENSITIVE WHISKERS

help the lion find its way in dense cover or on moonless nights. Moving in for the kill, it spreads its whiskers like a living circular net, which helps it select the best spot to clamp its great jaws on its victim.

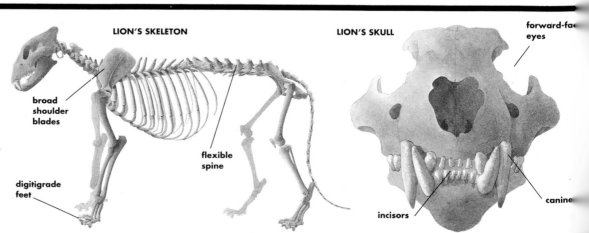

HEAD COMPARISON

In contrast to other cats—in which males and females, though differing in size, look very similar—adult male lions are easily distinguished from females because of their luxuriant manes.

SHORT HEAD

The face is much shorter and rounder than that of a wolf, hyena, or other carnivore, a result of the reduction in the length of the nasal cavity and a shortening of the jaws.

MANE

The mane of the male lion serves a dual function. It makes the lion look bigger and more imposing to rival males, giving an illusion of great size without the drawback of an increase in weight. It also provides the throat with padding in the event of a fight.

X RAY

The lion's skeleton is strong and sturdy and its spine very flexible, enabling its owner to combine agility with power. The shoulder blades are broad, providing attachment for the great muscles that power the shoulders and forelimbs. The collarbone is reduced to a thin sliver of bone, lodged within the shoulder muscles and free at either end; this helps the lion achieve a long stride when running after its prey.

LION'S SKELETON

broad shoulder blades

flexible spine

digitigrade feet

LION'S SKULL

forward-facing eyes

canine

incisors

X-ray illustrations Elisabeth Smith

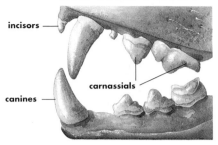

incisors

canines

carnassials

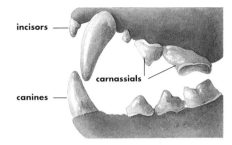

incisors

carnassials

canines

SCISSORLIKE TEETH

The lion uses its two pairs of greatly enlarged, cruelly pointed canine teeth to seize and throttle its prey. The small incisors, lying between the great canines, chop mouthfuls of flesh from the carcass. The molars and premolars are modified to form the carnassial teeth; their sharp cutting edges work against one another like shears to slice up prey.

HIND LIMBS

are sturdy and strongly muscled to provide power for the final sprint to catch prey and for leaping if necessary. A lion can run for short distances at about 40 mph (65 km/h) and leap up to 39 ft (12 m).

FORELIMBS

have powerfully developed muscles to enable the lion to knock down smaller prey with a single stroke and to seize and wrestle larger prey to the ground, where it can then give it a killing bite.

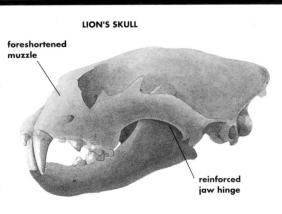

FACT FILE:

THE LION

CLASSIFICATION

GENUS: *PANTHERA*
SPECIES: *LEO*

SIZE

HEAD-BODY LENGTH/MALE: 8–9 FT (2.4–3.3 M)
HEAD-BODY LENGTH/FEMALE: 7–8 FT (2.3–2.6 M)
SHOULDER HEIGHT/MALE: UP TO 4 FT (1.2 M)
SHOULDER HEIGHT/FEMALE: UP TO 3.6 FT (1.1 M)
WEIGHT/MALE: 330–550 LB (150–240 KG)
WEIGHT/FEMALE: 270–300 LB (120–180 KG)
WEIGHT AT BIRTH: 2–4 LB (1.1–2 KG)

COLORATION

TYPICALLY PALE SANDY OR TAWNY YELLOW, BUT VARYING FROM GRAYISH BUFF TO YELLOWISH RED AND DARK OCHER; WHITE AROUND MOUTH AND ON CHIN, UNDERPARTS, AND INNER SIDES OF LEGS
MALE'S MANE DARK TAWNY, REDDISH BROWN, OR BLACK

FEATURES

TAIL, JUST OVER HALF THE LENGTH OF HEAD AND BODY, HAS LARGE TUFT OF LONG, BLACKISH HAIR AT TIP, WHICH CONCEALS A HORNY SPUR
MANE OF HAIRS IN MALE ONLY, UP TO 6.3 IN (16 CM) LONG ON SIDES OF FACE AND TOP OF HEAD, EXTENDING ON TO SHOULDERS, AROUND NECK, AND SHORT WAY DOWN SPINE
SHORT HAIR ON FACE, UPPER PARTS OF BODY, FLANKS, AND MOST OF TAIL; LONGER ON UNDERPARTS AND TAIL TIP
LONG, WHITISH WHISKERS ARRANGED IN PARALLEL ROWS ON SIDES OF UPPER LIP.
AMBER EYES AND BLACKISH NOSE; PROMINENT BLACK MARK AT BASE OF OUTSIDE OF ROUNDED EARS, USED IN VISUAL COMMUNICATION BETWEEN LIONS

SKULL

The lion's skull is massive, thick, and heavy, weighing up to 6 lb (3 kg). There are deep ridges and hollows to provide attachment for the huge muscles that power the jaw. The temporal muscle, running from the lower jaw to a flange at the rear of the skull, enables the lion to exert tremendous force when clamping its jaws.

LION'S SKULL

foreshortened muzzle

reinforced jaw hinge

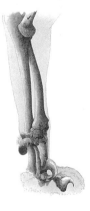

The outer bones of each toe, together with its claw, can be retracted into a fleshy sheath to create a padded paw for fast running (left). They are held in place by strong elastic ligaments. When the lion needs to extend its claws for attacking prey, in self-defense against a rival, or when climbing, flexor muscles straighten the outer toe bones so that the claws protrude (right).

PRIDE OF THE PACK

LIONS ARE THE MOST SOCIAL OF ALL THE CATS. THEY LEAD A COMMUNAL LIFE WHERE EQUALITY REIGNS: THE FEMALES PROVIDE AND THE MALES PROTECT

The lion is the only cat that lives permanently in mixed-sex groups. These groups, called prides, may range from large (up to forty members) to small (as few as four individuals). Each pride consists of one or more males and a larger number of females and their offspring.

However, not all lions live in prides. In harsher habitats such as the deserts of southwest Africa, where prey is much scarcer than on the savannas, lions live singly or in pairs. Also, within most populations, there are individuals that lead a nomadic life (see "The Wandering Life," page 1235).

A group of lionesses within a pride exhibit close cooperation when hunting together and an impressive degree of adaptability in stalking and capturing their prey. The great cats are able to respond quickly as conditions change from one minute to the next; they are able to improvize as the need arises.

Where undisturbed by tourism or other human interference, lions may be active by day, particularly in the morning and late afternoon when it is not too blisteringly hot. Especially where they are hunted or otherwise disturbed, however, they lead a predominantly nocturnal lifestyle, often with peaks of activity at dawn and dusk.

LAZY HAZY DAYS

Whatever the pattern they follow, lions, in common with the other cats, have a reputation as lazy animals and spend a great proportion of their time doing nothing. On average, they rest for about twenty or twenty-one hours out of twenty-four each day, sleeping soundly, dozing lightly, or merely staring into space. Even so, they can usually rouse themselves almost instantly when necessary.

Although they live in some of the hottest parts of the world, lions are not particularly well adapted to intense heat and spend much of their time lying in the shade of trees, rocks, thickets, and other cover. Sometimes they climb up into larger, more easily climbed trees to escape the fierce tropical sun and take advantage of any cool breezes. They drape their great bodies along the branches, moving only to follow the shade as the day passes.

TERRITORIAL HABITS

Each lion pride occupies a territory that it defends against intruders. The size of this territory depends on a variety of factors: the number of lions in the pride, the type of habitat, the abundance of prey, and the ease of catching it.

Within each pride, the lionesses normally remain in the territory for life, but the males stay

Purdy & Matthews/Survival Anglia

Lionesses rub heads (above) *before going hunting to reaffirm their bond as an organized unit.*

An adult male and cub (left) *crouch at a water hole to drink after they have finished eating.*

Jonathon Scott/Planet Earth Pictures

A lion marks the pride's territory by spraying a pungent mixture of urine and a secretion from its scent glands.

only for as long as they are able to defend themselves against strangers—rival males whose aim is to take over the pride. The male's main role in lion society is to protect the pride's territory, while the females do most of the hunting.

Living in a territory brings several major benefits. It reinforces group bonds, helping the pride members stick together, and reduces the possibility of chance encounters with hostile outsiders, which might lead to energy-wasting and damaging fights. Intimate knowledge of a particular area gives the pride members the best chance of finding and catching prey, as well as the safest sites for giving birth and hiding the cubs from other predators. All this knowledge can, in turn, be passed on from each pride member to the others, including the offspring, so that it becomes part of a shared culture and makes the pride a remarkably efficient unit.

In many areas, such as the Serengeti plains, it is not possible for lions to remain in a permanent territory all year. There simply is not enough prey and water to support them during the dry season. This means that the lions can occupy territories only along the edges of the plains and in the woodlands themselves. Fortunately, however, a pride does not claim a territory as its exclusive property, and the boundaries of most neighboring territories overlap. The lions avoid conflicts because a pride usually takes great care to trespass on a particular area within an adjacent pride's territory only when their neighbors are visiting another part of their domain. ■

Jonathon Scott/Planet Earth Pictures

HABITATS

Lions' favored habitats are grassy plains, savannas, open woodlands, and scrubland. Although they range over a wide variety of habitats, including semideserts and mountains (at heights of up to 16,400 ft/5,000 m in Kenya), they avoid dense forests. Unlike the largely solitary tiger and jaguar, which tend to take smaller prey and thrive in such closed habitats, lions are adapted to hunting cooperatively for bigger prey; these are very scarce in thick forests, and the members of a pride of lions would find it difficult to keep in touch in close cover.

Within the grassy plains and savannas, lions make use of big outcrops of rock called kopjes. These prominent landmarks make ideal sites for groups of lions or individuals to lie up, hidden from the view of humans and prey alike, and to move around so that they stay shaded from the fierce heat of the sun. They also use other large objects such as anthills for this purpose.

GREAT WANDERERS

Lions are great wanderers, and they may turn up from time to time in areas where they were previously unknown for many years—often in places a long way from their present limits of distribution. Every so often, for instance, a few individuals wander onto the livestock farmland of the Zimbabwe plateau, from where they were driven out many years before. These nomadic lions generally kill a few cattle and then vanish as mysteriously as they

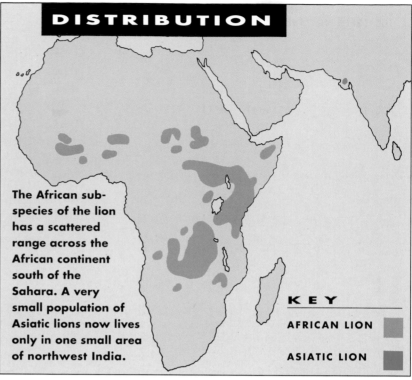

DISTRIBUTION

The African subspecies of the lion has a scattered range across the African continent south of the Sahara. A very small population of Asiatic lions now lives only in one small area of northwest India.

KEY

AFRICAN LION

ASIATIC LION

appear. Other wanderers have even ventured as far as the outskirts of large cities, such as Harare, the capital of Zimbabwe.

FOOD FOR ALL

The savanna grasslands are dominated by one group of plants: the grasses. Unlike many other flowering plants, the main growing parts of grasses are situated not at the tips of the stems, but at the bases of the leaves. This means that during the wet season, as fast as the great herds of zebras,

An Asiatic lion and subadults (left) *stop for refreshments in the Gir Forest Sanctuary on the Gujarat peninsula in northwest India.*

A pride of lions relaxes by water at the Ngorongoro Crater in Tanzania (right). *In arid habitats they survive on the water that occurs in the intestines or in the blood of prey.*

Joanne Vangruisen/Survival Anglia

Thomson's gazelles, and other grazing herbivores that wander these plains eat the leaves, the grasses grow again, thus providing a more or less continuous supply of food.

The east African savannas support the greatest remaining diversity and abundance of large grazing mammals in the world—over forty species of large grazing herbivores still live there, sharing a relatively uniform food supply. Rather than being spread evenly around the habitat, they mainly move in herds, constantly seeking nutritious new vegetation and water. During the dry season, when the savanna changes from a vast carpet of an intense green color to a parched, dusty expanse of rustling, dried-out, bleached-gold grass stems and leaves, huge numbers of wildebeests and other grazers are on the move, migrating from one area to another to find food and water.

DIFFERENT TACTICS

Although they all feed on the same food resource—grass—the many different species of grazers avoid competition by subtle differences in behavior. Three

major species of grazers follow one another across the savanna. Plains zebras are the first to graze the long grass, eating the tougher parts of the plants. This makes the rest of the grass available to blue wildebeests or brindled gnu, which crop the living carpet shorter. Finally the diminutive Thomson's gazelles eat the short sward that remains, supplementing their diet by browsing on acacia bushes. Other large herbivores, such as

> A PRIDE'S TERRITORY HAS A CENTER OF
> ACTIVITY—AN AREA IN WHICH IT CAN
> FIND MOST OF ITS FOOD AND WATER

giraffes and elephants, are browsers, feeding in different ways on the foliage of bushes and trees.

These huge herds of herbivorous mammals provide a rich source of food for a range of predators, including lions, leopards, cheetahs, spotted hyenas, and hunting dogs. Just as their prey's different feeding techniques prevent them from eating one another out of house and home, these predators generally avoid competition by each hunting a different range of prey in a different way.

THE LION'S SHARE

Although all five of the predators listed above hunt mammals weighing less than 220 lb (100 kg), only the lion habitually kills prey heavier than about 550 lb (250 kg). Also, lions take a greater proportion of healthy adult prey than do the other species.

Nicholas Parfitt/Tony Stone Worldwide

Lions specialize in hunting cooperatively, lying in wait for their prey at water holes or stalking it with great patience, using every available piece of cover in open habitats, until they are close enough to make a final brief dash. They are more successful when hunting at night.

Leopards, which are far smaller than lions but extremely strong and powerful predators nonetheless, tend to prey more on smaller creatures, such as Thomson's gazelles, wildebeest calves, and baboons. They hunt mainly in cover, especially in thickets and around kopjes, and are the supreme stalkers among the great cats.

Cheetahs—the most specialized of all the big cats—are by far the most lightly built of the great cats. Built for speed and not for stalking, they are the fastest of all land mammals. A hunting cheetah streaks across the open plains for short distances at speeds approaching 60 mph (100 km/h), running down Thomson's and other gazelles. In contrast to all other cats, it is almost entirely a daytime hunter.

PACK HUNTERS

The most powerful predator in Africa next to the lion is the spotted hyena. Once unjustly branded as a cowardly scavenger, it is bulky and powerful enough to attack wildebeest and other sizable

FOCUS ON

LIFE IN A NATIONAL PARK

Of all places where lions can be seen in numbers, the Serengeti National Park in Tanzania is a premier site. So many lions were being shot by big game hunters that the area was declared a game reserve in 1929. It became a national park in 1951, and in 1981 it—together with the adjacent Ngorongoro Conservation Area—was declared a World Heritage Site. It has been estimated that the total population of lions in the park needs to kill as much as 5,800 tons (5,890 tonnes) of prey every year to survive. This may seem like a great deal, but the predators do not endanger the continued existence of their prey. Lions, along with other predators, are an essential part of the savanna ecosystem, and the prey animals need the predators for survival just as much as the predators need the prey. The predators tend to take prey that is easier to catch, so that old, sick, or young animals are killed more often than healthy adults. Both predators and prey have shaped each other's evolutionary development. Prey has become fleet on foot, while the lions have attained a physical size and social structure ideally suited for exploiting a variety of large, grassland herbivores.

TEMPERATURE AND RAINFALL

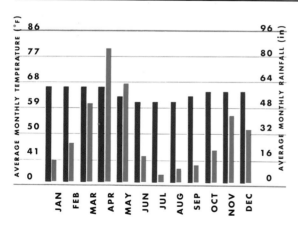

■ **TEMPERATURE**

■ **RAINFALL**

The Serengeti has an almost constant monthly temperature of 63–64°F (17–18°C) all year. After the November–May rainy season, the grasslands are arid, and most animals migrate elsewhere.

prey. And, like the lion, it has a highly evolved social system and is a very effective cooperative hunter. Packs of up to twenty-five spotted hyenas are capable of killing almost any prey, except for the real giants, such as elephants or rhinos.

Hunting dogs, though far less powerful, also benefit from hunting in packs. Capable of running fast for long periods, they can outpace and kill any sick or young animal, and sometimes tackle much larger healthy prey more than ten times their size, such as adult wildebeest or zebra. ■

NEIGHBORS

As well as immense populations of large grazing mammals and of lions and other predators, the Serengeti region supports a wealth of other animals and a rich plant life.

AFRICAN ELEPHANT

The African elephant is a generalist grazer, feeding on a wide range of plants according to availability.

DUNG BEETLE

Dung beetles perform a vital service by breaking down animal droppings, on which their larvae feed.

Illustrations Kim Thompson

SERENGETI NATIONAL PARK

Containing the greatest concentrations of large wild animals in the world, Serengeti National Park covers 5,708 square miles (14,783 square kilometers)—about three times the size of the Grand Canyon National Park. It lies in Tanzania, to the east of Lake Victoria, and extends as far north as Kenya.

KENYA

Serengeti National Park

TANZANIA

Purdy & Matthews/Survival Anglia

RUPPELL'S GRIFFON VULTURE

This vulture is one of several vulture species that feast on the abundant carrion of the savanna.

CHEETAH

Cheetahs are vulnerable to other large predators, such as lions, which steal their prey and eat their cubs.

RED-BILLED QUELEA

Flocks of up to a million of these birds follow the rains, stripping the grain from crops.

COMMON JACKAL

Black-backed jackal pups are often guarded by adult "baby-sitters," usually their older siblings.

BLACK RHINO

The black rhino uses its highly mobile, elongated upper lip to pull leaves into its mouth.

HUNTING

When they are not dozing contentedly, lions spend much of their time scanning the great expanse of the savanna, following the movements of their prey. Often, pride members will rest near a herd of grazing mammals, watching them from time to time but making no move to attack. Then, as the bloodred disk of the sun sinks below the horizon and the lions' tawny bodies melt into their surroundings, they begin to stalk their prey. Although lions will make kills in daylight—if they get the opportunity—they usually hunt under cover of darkness. Their success rate in bringing down prey is considerably greater at night and when pride members cooperate in the hunt.

The majority of lions live in prides, and within a pride it is the lionesses that do almost all of the hunting. The males rarely join in, remaining in the background and generally keeping out of the way until the hunt is over. This has given them an undeserved reputation for laziness. In fact, it would not be to the pride's advantage for a male to participate in the hunt. His main job is to defend the territory against rivals. His heavy bulk makes him slower and less agile than the lionesses, and his conspicuous bushy mane reduces his chances of surprising prey. An added bonus is that, by dropping to the rear, he can protect the cubs that also remain behind. By contrast, solitary nomad males do have to catch and scavenge their own food; they generally do not do as well as lions living in prides.

OPPORTUNISTIC HUNTERS

Although lions readily scavenge carcasses they come across or forcibly commandeer, they hunt most of their food themselves. They are opportunistic hunters, taking a wide range of prey from mice to buffalo and ostriches to pythons. One study in the Serengeti found that the lions there ate twenty-two different kinds of prey.

Despite this, lions do have preferences. They do not usually bother to chase diminutive prey such as hares and small birds because of the poor return on the energy required to catch them. At the other end of the size scale, they are generally reluctant to tackle very large, well-armed prey, such as elephants and rhinos, unless they come across

an unprotected youngster or a sick or injured adult.

In general, lions chiefly go for medium-sized animals, in the 100–1,000 lb (45–450 kg) weight range, concentrating on those they can catch most easily. Wildebeests and zebras are still abundant in areas such as the Serengeti and fit the bill exactly. Other medium-sized prey on the lion's menu include topi, impala, eland, reedbuck, and waterbuck. Such animals are relatively easy for a small group of lions or even a loner to kill, yet they provide enough meat for several lions to share. Large groups of lions can tackle giraffes, buffalo, and other big and potentially dangerous prey.

Their diet varies from one region to another, depending on what is available locally. Thus the lions in Kruger National Park, South Africa, eat large numbers of impalas, while in Kafue National Park, Zambia, buffalo, hartebeest, and warthogs feature prominently on the menu of the local lions. The choice of prey also varies with the season and opportunities at the time.

The antelopes and other large herbivores that form the bulk of the lion's prey are fast runners, capable of sustaining speeds of up to 50 mph (80 km/h). Their pursuers, by contrast, can reach a speed of about 30–35 mph (49–57 km/h) only over

THE AMBUSH
The hunting party (right) fans out in a broad front to cover as much ground as possible. Once prey is sighted, the lionesses on the flanks move forward and creep around behind the prey. They may rush the prey, stampeding it into the path of the main group.

A successful hunt is far from guaranteed. The zebra (below) is putting up a brave fight, and it may even gallop to freedom.

PREY IS SIGHTED
and the female moves forward cautiously, stalking her victim.

ON THE ALERT
A lioness holds her head up while she is on the lookout for prey.

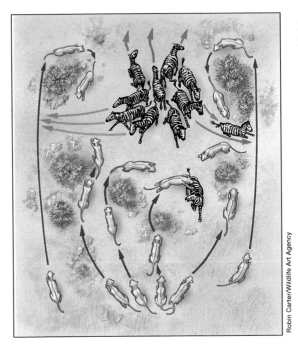

Robin Carter/Wildlife Art Agency

lion's patience may be rewarded; if the prey has not already spotted its pursuer and taken flight, the lion will be able to get close enough to its quarry to make a final deadly rush. The great cat suddenly bursts from cover, approaching from behind or alongside the startled quarry. If it can, it will get close enough to the prey to spring on its back, but it may have to run after it. Most chases are brief—330–990 ft (100–300 m) at most—and the lion may be able to cover 330 ft (100 m) in as little as six seconds.

The aim is to throw the prey off its feet and subdue it as quickly as possible. With the majority of medium-sized prey, such as wildebeests or zebras, the lion rakes one of its giant forepaws over the animal's rump with such force that it knocks it over, or it may sink its terrible claws into the victim's back and use its weight and great muscular strength to drag it down. Once the prey is down, there is little chance of escape. ■

BRINGING DOWN THE PREY

When the time is right, the lion will go in for the kill. Sometimes, a lion will ride on the back of the prey until it buckles under the weight.

short distances. This means that the lions generally rely on stealth rather than speed to catch their prey.

Lions are superb stalkers, using the slightest cover—such as a small shrub or tuft of grass—to conceal themselves as they approach their intended victims. When a lion has spotted suitable prey, it moves toward it purposefully but carefully, eyes fixed firmly on the target. It moves rapidly when the prey is feeding, drinking, or resting, and "freezes," motionless, whenever the prey looks up or shows any signs of nervousness. As the lion nears the prey, it becomes more and more alert and holds its head and body close to the ground. Eventually, after a stalk lasting up to several hours, the

CROUCHING

under cover, the lioness waits for the moment to give chase.

PREY

The lion stuns small prey with a swipe of its forepaw. It kills larger prey by clamping its jaws on the windpipe, which suffocates it.

PORCUPINE

THOMSON'S GAZELLE

WILDEBEEST

Ruth Grewcock

SOCIAL STRUCTURE

Although a small proportion of lions live as nomads, very few lions live a solitary life. Young males may spend some time roaming in bachelor parties of several individuals, but the great majority of adults live in family groups, or prides.

BLOOD TIES

Lionesses form the nucleus of lion society. Typically, there are from four to twelve lionesses in a pride. The cubs borne by the lionesses generally stay in the pride if they are females; male cubs, however, leave of their own accord or are driven out by the pride male or males when subadult, or about two or three years old. All the females of a pride are therefore related to one another, usually comprising a group of sisters and their daughters—and sometimes also their granddaughters. Unrelated lionesses are not allowed to join the pride.

There are usually from one to six adult males in each pride. They may be related to one another—some may be brothers: others, half brothers, cousins, or more distant relatives. In contrast to the lionesses, the males do not remain in the same pride permanently. Some stay for as little as six months, others as long as six years or even more—depending on the number of males in the pride, and hence their collective strength, and on the severity of competition from rival males—but all eventually leave. Occasionally they wander off of their own accord, but generally they are driven from the pride by stronger rival males. These rivals are the males driven out of another pride when young, perhaps with the odd single male, that wander around until they have

A MALE LION
wrinkles his nose (left) *after smelling the urine of a rival.*

HOSTILITY
Lions have expressive faces, especially when showing hostility (above).

LIONS' LANGUAGE

Lions have a rich and varied language. They signal their intentions with a variety of methods, involving facial expressions, tail movements, and other body language such as touching and grooming between same-sex individuals. They also communicate through scent marking and can produce an amazing variety of growls, meows, moans, grunts, and hisses. Cubs can produce a delightful soft sound when content.

HISSING
(above) *is just one of a variety of sounds used by lions when communicating.*

THE LION'S ROAR

(above) *has numerous variations, from the soft contact call to the famous full-throated sound.*

WARNING SIGNALS

A lioness will snarl in annoyance to discourage a friendly cub from unwanted boisterous antics.

BARING TEETH

A lion uses this gesture to threaten an intruder or when it is frightened.

DIVIDE AND RULE

A pride is often split into smaller subprides or companionships, which operate in different areas within the pride's territory.

INFANTICIDE BY MALES

When a male takes over control of a pride, he usually kills the cubs that were fathered by the ousted leader. The females will come into heat sooner than if they had cubs to raise. The new male will then mate with the females as quickly as possible, passing on his own genes.

Richard Matthews/Planet Earth Pictures

FEMALE THREAT

This expression (below) is at its most intense when the female is fiercely guarding her kill.

grown large and strong enough to challenge the male or males of a pride and take their place. The pride they take over is unlikely to be the one in which they grew up, so the pride males are not usually related to the females.

This constantly changing pattern, with new males replacing older ones, results in a good gene flow and prevents inbreeding.

SOCIAL STATUS

The lionesses within a pride do not seem to have any sort of hierarchy among themselves, although they tend to give way to a male when feeding at a kill. However, even a large, powerful male may give way to three or four determined females.

The male lions within a pride are usually the best of friends; although they will defend the pride fiercely from strange males, they do not often seem to fight each other over the right to mate with females. Because all the females in a pride typically come into heat at the same time, such competition is usually avoided. The males generally stick to a sort of gentlemen's agreement, by which the first male to approach a female in heat is accepted by the other males as having dominance with regard to mating. It is to the males' advantage not to fight. Apart from the risk of injury or death, it is not a disaster if a male allows his pride companion to mate in his place, since the two are likely to be closely related, and so some of his own genes will be passed on to the next generation anyway. Also, males need to stick together if they can, since larger groups of males are able to maintain possession of a pride for much longer than a pair of males or a single lion. ∎

All illustrations John Morris/Wildlife Art Agency

LIFE CYCLE

Lions usually become sexually mature between three and four years of age, although they may not finish growing until they are six years old.

Females come into heat more than once a year at irregular intervals, for three to five days (or more) each time. In some areas, however, most or all of the females in a pride tend to give birth at about the same time—which often coincides with the time when their prey are rearing young.

Males approach receptive females after detecting a distinctive scent in their urine. While he is courting her, a male will remain close to a female for several days on end. She may tease the male, rolling over on her back and slapping at him playfully with one of her great paws, then running off, returning to rub noses, and bounding away again.

Mating itself lasts about a minute and takes place frequently. A pair may mate every twenty minutes or so, day and night, for as long as five days. During the time she is in heat, a female may mate with several of the pride males. The male of the mating pair licks the female frequently on the shoulder, neck, or back and gently bites her neck, to which she responds by grunting gently.

LIFE BEGINS

After an average gestation period of 110 days, the cubs are born, weighing a mere 2–4 lb (1–2 kg) each. When their eyes open, within two weeks, they are blue-gray; they do not change to the distinctive amber color until the cubs are two to three months old.

At birth, they have soft, woolly, grayish yellow fur, covered in pale spots. Their coats become sleeker and lose their spots after three to five months, though the cubs may not lose the spots on their sides and legs until they are fully grown.

The cubs' first teeth appear when they are about three weeks old. At this age, they can walk reasonably well, but before then, their mother may need to move them from one hiding place to another if she is suspicious or disturbed. She will gently pick up each cub in her great mouth by the scruff of its neck and carry it, the cub hanging limply with its legs drawn up to its chin. Small cubs are highly vulnerable to predators, such as jackals, leopards, and hyenas—and strange male lions. When their mother leaves to hunt, they spend most of their time hiding silently among rocks or concealed in vegetation. The lioness

A young cub chews on bark, which helps keep its teeth and gums strong and healthy.

Illustrations Robin Budden/Wildlife Art Agency

MATING

There is little real aggression during mating. Snarling, roaring, or growling seem to be part of the ritual.

YOUNG BLOOD

While learning hunting skills, older cubs may be lucky and catch themselves a young gazelle or smaller prey.

Tony Stone Worldwide

GROWING UP

The life of a young lion

NEWBORN CUBS

The tiny cubs, born with their eyes closed, are helpless and barely able to crawl.

EATING OUT

Cubs can feed even if their own mother's milk has dried up or if she is temporarily absent, because other suckling lionesses share feeding duties.

may spend twenty-four hours or more away from her cubs.

When they are about two months old, the cubs begin to follow their mother on her expeditions, and if they have been reared mainly alone, they must learn to socialize with the rest of the pride. Other lionesses may allow cubs to suckle from them. This unusual behavior makes sense because, no matter who the cubs' mother is, she will be a relative of the other lionesses, and her offspring will carry some of the same genes.

Weaning is a gradual process. By the time they are about two and a half to three months old, the cubs are given their first taste of meat. They are taken to a kill, where they are allowed small scraps of flesh. They eat increasing amounts of meat, but continue to suckle until they are about six months old. They do not participate in kills until they are at least a year old. By 14 to 15 months, they have lost all their milk teeth and start to grow the large canines they will need to capture and kill prey. The youngsters remain entirely dependent on the adults for food until they are 16 months old. About two months later, their mother stops leading them to kills and caring for them in other ways, letting them stand on their own within the pride. Soon, she will give birth to more young. On average, females produce a litter of cubs every two years, and may continue to do so until they are fifteen years old. ∎

PLAY FIGHTING

helps older cubs develop muscles and learn skills that will be essential later in life, when they will have to tackle large prey to the ground or fight intruders or rivals.

FROM BIRTH TO DEATH

THE LION

GESTATION: 100–119 DAYS (TYPICALLY 105–110 DAYS)

LITTER SIZE: 1–5 (USUALLY 3–4); UP TO 6 IN CAPTIVITY

BREEDING: ANY TIME OF YEAR, THOUGH IN SOME AREAS MORE CUBS MAY BE BORN IN SOME SEASONS THAN IN OTHERS

WEIGHT AT BIRTH: 2–4 LB (1–2 KG)

EYES OPEN: 3–15 DAYS

FIRST WALKING: 3 WEEKS

WEANING: ABOUT 6 MONTHS

SEXUAL MATURITY: 3–4 YEARS

LONGEVITY: UP TO 17 YEARS IN THE WILD; UP TO 24 YEARS IN CAPTIVITY

THE LIONS' SHARE

LIONS HAVE LONG ENJOYED A PROMINENT PLACE IN HISTORY, BUT HISTORY IS EXACTLY WHAT THEY ARE DESTINED TO BECOME UNLESS ADEQUATE MEASURES ARE TAKEN TO PRESERVE THEIR HOMELAND

Except for humans, domestic animals, and wild species (such as rats) that have benefited from human settlement, lions in their heyday were the most widespread of all land mammals.

Until about ten thousand years ago, lions ranged over most of Africa, almost all of Eurasia, and throughout North America, Central America, and into northern South America. As dense forests appeared in much of Europe, the lion gradually disappeared from this part of its range. Its demise was hastened by the appearance of advanced human hunters, who competed with lions for the large herbivorous mammals on which both preyed.

By about two thousand years ago, the last lions had disappeared from the Balkans—their last main stronghold in Europe—and from Palestine by the time of the Crusades. Since then, lions have been reduced to a fragment of their former range and numbers, because as humans and their agriculture spread worldwide, the mighty cats were branded as predators of livestock and killed on sight.

A PLACE IN HISTORY

Few other animals have suffered such a dramatic shrinking of range during historical times as the lion. And yet few have made such a deep and lasting impression on human consciousness and imagination. From the earliest times, the lion was regarded as a symbol of courage and given the title King of the Beasts.

In ancient Egypt, statues depicted pharaohs with lions' bodies, and the Assyrian kings were represented as giant, winged lions with human heads. Stone lions have guarded palaces and other great buildings the world over for many hundreds of years. The lion has also played a major part in heraldry, appearing on numerous coats of arms. Masai warriors wore lions' manes as a symbol of strength and bravery. Today, this great cat is common not only as the star of wildlife movies, African safaris, and zoos, but also in cartoons, advertisements, and other popular images.

HUNTED BY MAN

Lion hunting has long been common. The first historical records date back as far as the days of ancient Egypt, when the Pharaoh Amenhotep III (1417–1379 B.C.) killed more than one hundred lions during his ten-year rule. Later, Assyrian hunters used horse-drawn chariots to pursue lions, many of them bred specially for the purpose. The Romans were famous for their fascination with lions, organizing major hunting expeditions to capture these and other great cats. Lions were often pitted against gladiators in elaborate battles, and prisoners were thrown to them, providing gruesome

Joanne Vangruisen/Survival Anglia

An Asiatic lioness and cub (above). *This subspecies is now reduced to one area in northwest India.*

Joanne Vangruisen/Survival Anglia

THEN & NOW

This map shows the former and present ranges of both the African and the Asiatic lions.

/// **FORMER**   ▨ **PRESENT**

The lion once roamed over virtually every part of Africa and from southeastern Europe through the Middle East into all of northern India. Today, however, the picture is very different. The African lion is now restricted to scattered conservation areas south of the Sahara, while the Asiatic lion has suffered even greater losses. It has disappeared from most of its former range and now occurs only in the Gir Forest Sanctuary in Gujarat, northern India.

entertainment for the rulers and masses alike.

Lions have been hunted ever since—by farmers and others who saw the lion as a dangerous predator of their livestock and, especially during the Victorian era, by game hunters.

One of the largest races of the lion, the Barbary lion of North Africa, was wiped out by hunters. By the 1890s it was gone from Tunisia and was almost wiped out in Algeria, too. Its final stronghold was the Atlas Mountains—hence an alternative name for the subspecies, the Atlas lion. Here, the last wild Barbary lion was shot in 1922. As well as being the largest of modern lions, adult male Barbary lions had the most impressive manes, extending down the middle of the body and on to the underparts. There may be a few genes from

Hunted throughout history, lions are now free to roam in established conservation areas.

ENDANGERED SPECIES

Barbary lions in some of the hybrid stock kept in zoo collections, but the wild Barbary lion will roam no more.

At the other end of the African continent, a similar fate befell the Cape lion. Its mane was almost as impressive as that of its North African relative, only it was black. Although its exact range is uncertain, it is known that the last Cape lion was killed in Natal in 1865.

In India, too, Asiatic lions were slaughtered in great numbers. Lion hunting was very fashionable in the days of the British Raj—one army officer shot fourteen lions in ten days.

A PRECARIOUS EXISTENCE

As with the other big cats, lions are top predators in their range and are thus highly vulnerable to extinction if the numbers of their prey fall below a certain critical level. Prey numbers, in their turn, are dependent on such factors as poaching and dwindling food resources as humans and their livestock compete for space. Furthermore, because they are—understandably—feared and hated by farmers and other local people, it is possible for lions in an area to be wiped out before their habitat is destroyed.

Although the behavior of the lion is among the most thoroughly studied of all wild animals, there is relatively little information available on

---

THE AFRICAN LION IS NOT THREATENED WITH EXTINCTION, BUT ITS LONG-TERM SURVIVAL IS FAR FROM ASSURED

---

its distribution, numbers, and population dynamics in Africa. Far more is known about tiger numbers than those of lions, despite the fact that tigers are much more secretive animals and live in dense cover. Studies currently under way should partly help fill in the gaps in our knowledge, but there is much to be learned before it is too late.

Population estimates are approximate, but it is thought that there are between 6,000 and 9,000 lions in southern Africa, south of the Zambezi River. Of this number, over 4,000 individuals are protected in reserves. Although the lion is rare in West Africa, several thousand still exist in East Africa, and much of this population seems to be relatively stable. However, there is no cause for complacency: Even though hunting is regulated, many lions are still killed illegally by farmers and poachers using guns and poison or are trapped in snares set for other animals. More serious, rapidly growing populations mean less space for the lions—and more competition for food with humans.

Popperfoto

ASIATIC LIONS

Despite the problems facing the African lion, the situation with the Asiatic subspecies (*Panthera leo persica*) is far more perilous. In historic times, Asiatic, or Asian, lions ranged from Greece to central India; but by 1900 hunting and agricultural expansion caused the population to be reduced to under 100 individuals. With protection, numbers slowly climbed to 180 by 1970. Today, the last remnants of the Asiatic lion population are slightly more numerous, having been built up by careful conservation to almost 300 animals, but the subspecies is still threatened.

The chief problem is that the entire population of wild Asiatic lions lives in just one small reserve with an area of 540 square miles (1,400 square kilometers)—the Gir Forest Sanctuary in northwest India. Here, the increasing incidence of encounters between lions and the local people is posing a major dilemma. Periodic droughts reduce the numbers of the lions' natural prey, and the predators must then turn their attentions to cattle, goats, and other domestic animals. A really long period of drought could result in the lions' starving to death.

As with all small and highly localized populations of wild animals, the damaging effects of inbreeding could pose a problem for the Asiatic lion. Also, with the growth of the lion population and the fact that they do not always remain

CONSERVATION MEASURES

● The Indian Forestry Commission has initiated a program of reintroduction of some of the Gir Forest lions to other areas. As well as potential problems with local people, they have had to take into account the need to find a large enough area of habitat suitable for lions, containing plenty of prey. The reintroduction site must also contain no tigers, as these would compete with the lions. Finally, it is vital that the conveniently within the sanctuary's borders, they have made more attacks on humans.

If there is any breakdown in the system of protection given to the lions, the animals are put at risk as local people take the law into their own hands. This happened in 1987, when the sanctuary guards went on strike and several lions were killed.

Finally, being concentrated in just one small area means that the Gir Forest lions would be highly vulnerable to extinction should disease strike.

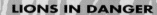

Inset picture Vivec Singh/Survival Anglia

LIONS IN DANGER

ASIATIC LION	ENDANGERED

ENDANGERED MEANS THAT THE ANIMAL IS IN DANGER OF EXTINCTION AND THAT ITS SURVIVAL IS UNLIKELY UNLESS STEPS ARE TAKEN TO SAVE IT.

ALTHOUGH THE AFRICAN LION IS NOT THREATENED OR ENDANGERED AS A SPECIES, ONLY ABOUT 10 PERCENT OF INDIVIDUALS SURVIVE TO OLD AGE. BESIDES DYING FROM STARVATION OR INJURY, LIONS SUFFER EITHER DIRECTLY OR AS A RESULT OF INFECTION FROM PARASITES AND DISEASES. TICKS MAY CARRY PARASITES SUCH AS BABESIA, WHICH BREAKS DOWN THE LION'S BLOOD CELLS AND CAN PROVE FATAL. LIONS HAVE BEEN KNOWN TO CONTRACT ANTHRAX AFTER EATING THE MEAT OF DISEASED PREY.

ASIATIC LIONS RELAXING IN THE GIR FOREST SANCTUARY IN THE INDIAN STATE OF GUJARAT.

lions stay in the reserve after they have been moved there, otherwise the exercise will have been in vain.

● In 1929 the vast Serengeti area of Tanzania was declared a game reserve. It became a national park in 1951. In 1981—together with the adjacent Ngorongoro Conservation Area—the region was declared a World Heritage Site. Both areas are home to large populations of lions.

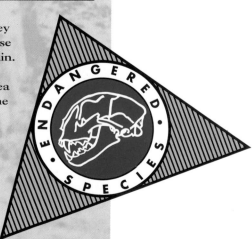

One of the most poignant losses was the disappearance of the lion population of Skeleton Coast Park, Namibia, in southwest Africa. Although these animals had evolved the ability to survive the harsh conditions by eating fur seals, they were then wiped out by farmers. Restocking the park will require careful selection of healthy animals that will be likely to adapt to the tough environment.

CAPTIVE BREEDING

Although lions had long been kept in captivity, there was little real understanding of how to encourage them to breed successfully until the second half of the 19th century. Lions kept at London Zoo were still being fed only joints of meat, and were thus deprived of the hair, skin, and guts—and the vitamins and minerals they contain—they would have consumed in the wild. It was realized that diet might be partly responsible for the poor breeding record of the lions in the zoo, and their diet was changed to include whole small animals and a supplement of bone meal.

Another reason for the difficulties with breeding lions in captivity was that the females were denied secluded dens in which to rear their cubs free from interruptions and the gaze of the visiting public. As soon as these two main problems were addressed, lions in zoos began to breed regularly and in good numbers. With the great proliferation of smaller zoos and safari parks in the 1960s, however, too many lions were soon being produced.

Shipping these surplus animals to Africa and liberating them in the wild might seem to be an attractive answer, but, as so often with conservation issues, the reality is not so simple. The release of large, captive-bred carnivores is beset with problems, which are only beginning to be solved. For example, many safe areas in Africa

ALONGSIDE MAN

MAN-EATING LIONS

Although lions usually give humans a wide berth—with good reason, considering they have been persecuted for thousands of years—they will sometimes attack people, and a few become regular man-eaters. Occasionally rogue individuals, often sick or starving, kill humans, but generally several members of a pride are involved. The most famous of these were the so-called man-eaters of Tsavo, which accounted for forty people working on the Mombasa-to-Kampala railroad in a single year. In 1898 these men were building the bridge and laying the rails over the Tsavo River, in Kenya, when the lions made repeated attacks. Two of the man-eaters were finally shot by Colonel Patterson, the leading engineer, but sporadic attacks continued in the area. On one occasion a particularly bold lion forced its way into a train car and killed a police inspector who had been waiting to surprise it but had fallen asleep! Another infamous group of fifteen lions, representing two generations, killed and ate people regularly around Nombe in southern Tanzania during the early 1930s. Before they were shot in 1947, they were estimated to have killed as many as 1,000 to 1,500 people. As with the Tsavo man-eaters, they appeared to be in excellent condition and were surrounded by an abundance of other game.

where lions occur, such as national parks and game reserves, do not contain sufficient prey to sustain larger populations. So zoos have found it necessary to control the numbers of captive-bred lions. They have used a mixture of methods to achieve this goal.

BIRTH CONTROL

Keeping the sexes separate might be a simple enough solution for solitary predators, but not one that suits the intensely social lion. Instead, one of the chief ways of keeping the captive lion population down to a manageable level is by the use of birth control.

Vasectomies are routinely carried out on male lions—though the animal undergoes the risks of being sedated under general anesthetic. Despite the simplicity of the operation, which in humans is usually carried out under local anesthetic, few lions will allow themselves to be interfered with unless they are fully unconscious. Another difficulty with this method is that it is not really possible to reverse a vasectomy, so the vasectomized males are lost forever as potential breeding stock.

The other birth control method does not suffer from this drawback. Contraceptive implants can be given to lions in the form of a small cylinder inserted beneath a lioness's skin, usually in the hind leg, under general anesthetic. The implant—smaller than a tube of lipstick—seems to cause the animal no discomfort and remains effective for eighteen months to two years before it needs to be replaced. Whenever the female is required for breeding, it is a simple matter to remove the implant. However, there is a problem with this method, too. Lionesses that have carried the implants within their bodies for long periods of time show an increased chance of developing cancer of the reproductive tract.

CULLING CUBS

Another method of regulating lion numbers in zoos is euthanasia of cubs, generally at about two years of age. Although it is unpopular with the public, it is similar to the situation in the wild, where the great majority of cubs die (often after suffering starvation or disease). However, coordinated and scientifically managed population plans—such as the Species Survival Plan in North America—employ contraception effectively and offer the preferred option for avoiding surplus cubs. ■

Today, safaris in Africa's national parks and game reserves are for camera-wielding tourists instead of the gun-toting big game hunters of yesteryear.

Stephen Krasemann/NHPA

INTO THE FUTURE

To date, most work on lion conservation has been done on the tiny, critically endangered wild population of Asiatic lions that hangs on in the Gir Forest Sanctuary in India. However, African lions are increasingly being studied as the need to manage them increases.

The lion population of Etosha Park in Namibia, southwest Africa—the world's densest—has already been carefully monitored and managed in an effort to stabilize their numbers so that they do not eat themselves into starvation. The digging of new boreholes for water to attract wildlife has given the lions the chance to eat too many of their prey. Outbreaks of the disease anthrax have also caused large die-offs of prey.

Contraceptive implants and injections have been used at Etosha with generally good results. The lionesses' behavior as well as their medical condition

PREDICTION

PRESERVING POPULATIONS

Although the short-term outlook for the African race of the lion is far less bleak than that facing the tiger, it, too, is likely to face extinction unless action is taken now to preserve adequate amounts of suitable habitat.

has been carefully monitored, and any changes that might affect them adversely, such as an alteration in pride structure, have been recorded.

As with tigers, lions face an increasing problem in that these great predators are too large and too competitive with humans to coexist anywhere but in reserves where they can receive total protection and management.

THREATENED HABITATS

But the problem is that there are not enough reserves large enough to support the numbers of prey—and of lions—that will ensure that healthy stocks of the great cats can be maintained for the future. Even the inadequate reserves that do exist are coming under ever-increasing pressure as the human population grows at an alarming rate. The demand for more land to grow more food and create industries to provide a higher standard of living will mean that more and more areas suitable for lions and other wildlife will be lost. ■

PUREBRED PROBLEMS

Until recently, it was thought that the population of some two hundred Asian lions in European and American zoos represented a vital pure stock of these animals for continued captive-breeding programs and future reintroductions to the wild, thus saving the subspecies even if the wild population in the Gir Forest were wiped out by some calamity. However, molecular analysis of these captive lions showed that all but a very few of them were hybrids. The gene pool has been diluted by a particularly prolific pair of hybrid lions that were among the mere seven or so lions that founded the entire zoo population. This meant that the years of captive breeding were to no avail, since the four or five pure Asian lions were too old for successful breeding.

In an attempt to fix the situation, a new breeding program has been started using animals from Sakkarbaug Zoo, near the Gir Forest. This zoo specializes in breeding pure Asian lions (the stock is regularly augmented by wild animals taken from the Gir Sanctuary that are injured or have caused problems with the local people by attacking them or eating their livestock) and supplying them to other zoos. In December 1990 London Zoo received the first consignment of four purebred Asian lions, two males and two females—the first group to be sent out of Asia for almost twenty years. The captive-breeding program will continue, with more animals being sent out to other Western zoos.

FOSTER PARENTS

Recently, success has been obtained with the fostering of Asian lion cubs at London Zoo. The cubs, whose mother was unable to rear them, were first hand-fed by keepers and then gradually introduced to a foster mother and her two cubs. After a tense period when there was a risk of the animals fighting, the cubs settled down with their new parent. Such techniques address the concern that zoo professionals have for rearing young animals as naturally as possible so that they adjust appropriately to their own species.

Illustration Evi Antoniou

LYNX & WILDCATS

Konrad Wothe/Oxford Scientific Films

A SECRET
SUCCESS

RADIATING EAST AND WEST FROM A CRADLE OF ORIGIN IN ASIA,
A NUMBER OF SMALL CAT SPECIES HAVE SECRETIVELY—BUT
SUCCESSFULLY—COLONIZED MUCH OF EUROPE AND ASIA

A mid the purple heather blanketing the high country of northeast Scotland, a dog has paused during a walk across the moors and is now barking excitedly. The source of its agitation turns out to be a cat, similar to a large domestic tabby, backed up against an outcrop of lichen-covered granite.

But it is not behaving as most cats do when confronted by a dog. Instead of snarling and arching its back while raising the hair all over its body, it first crouches down, with its tail lowered. Then it rears up on its forelegs to make itself look as big as possible. With ears pressed flat against its head, it growls a deep, ceaseless warning, and as the dog pushes its nose forward to investigate, it spits ferociously. This is the Eurasian wildcat. It is a truly wild animal, not a feral descendant of domestic stock, and was once found over much of Britain, as well as in many other parts of the world. In the United Kingdom it is now confined to remote areas of Scotland.

CLASSIFICATION

All cats belong to the Felidae family. The small cats were once listed within several different genera; today most zoologists place them all in the genus Felis, but may group them together under the Felinae subfamily. Ten of these species are found only in the New World.

ORDER

Carnivora
(carnivores)

FAMILY

Felidae
(felids—cats)

SUBFAMILY

Felinae

GENUS

Felis

SPECIES

thirty

1251

The marbled cat (below) *has a sumptuously dense coat and looks similar to a small clouded leopard.*

Terry Whittaker/Frank Lane Picture Agency

The small cats, though far less well known than their larger relatives, total some thirty species scattered across the Americas, Africa, Europe, and Asia. They are absent only from Antarctica, the Australian interior, and a few islands such as Madagascar. This volume concerns the thirteen species found from northern Britain across Eurasia to the southeast Asian islands of Indonesia and the Philippines. These are the Eurasian wildcat, lynx, jungle cat, Asiatic golden cat, Chinese desert cat, Pallas's cat, rusty-spotted cat, bay cat, fishing cat, marbled cat, leopard cat, flat-headed cat, and Iriomote cat.

THE MIACIDS

Like all carnivores, cats originated in a group of tree-dwelling animals called miacids that lived some 50 million years ago. From them, the modern carnivore families evolved and radiated, with animals recognizable as ancestral cats appearing around 40 million

A wildcat meticulously grooms its soft, thick coat in order to maintain the coat's insulating qualities.

Manfred Danegger/NHPA

(in) SIGHT

ISLAND CATS

It is very unusual to find cats that are native only to islands, as opposed to those that have been introduced. Two such native species are the bay cat and the Iriomote cat. Found only on the island of Borneo, the bay cat has a rusty brown or gray coat. The Iriomote cat was only described scientifically at the end of the 1960s; many authorities consider it to be the most primitive of all wild species. Found only on the small island of Iriomote, east of Taiwan, it is unusual in having partially webbed toes and semiretractile claws. It is similar in size to a domestic cat, but it has shorter legs; dark rows of spots run along its dark brown coat. Its short tail is thick and bushy with dark rings.

The adaptable leopard cat has colonized a number of islands, including the Japanese island of Tsushima, where it is known as the Tsushima cat. It is a little smaller and darker than leopard cats found elsewhere.

---

years ago. By 24 million years ago, cats of the subfamily Felinae—still the present-day classification for small cats—had appeared. For the next 20 million years, the cat family was dominated by the saber-toothed cats. These had massive canine teeth in the upper jaw, which they used to stab and pierce their prey. They were to die out as the ponderous animals that they preyed upon were replaced by modern hoofed mammals.

EARLY EXPANSION

Some zoologists believe that modern cats evolved through three major lineages: The first gave rise to the small South American cats, the second to the small cats of Europe and Asia, and the third to all the remaining cat species. In prehistoric times the cats were myriads more numerous and spread over wider areas than today. Landmasses were a different shape, with varying vegetation and climates; as these changed, cats became separated and continued to evolve according to their particular environmental conditions.

The Asiatic golden cat, for example, is very similar and obviously closely related to the African golden cat, although they are now found some 4,300 miles (7,000 km) apart. It is thought that at one time there was a stretch of moist forest reaching from Africa to tropical Asia. This was home to golden cats. Then, as the climate became drier in the central area, the cats became separated geographically by hot deserts, which were environmentally unfriendly as far as cats were concerned. As a result, the one species of golden cat became split into two and ultimately developed into two distinct species.

The lynx is another whose early wanderings have led to a wide separation of the species, for it is found in western Europe across much of Eurasia and also in Canada and the northern United States. However, unlike the African and Asiatic golden cats, which are now recognized as two species, the lynx is generally regarded as the same species in all parts of the range, even though there may be some regional differences in size and coat color.

CAT CHARACTERISTICS

All members of the cat family share certain basic characteristics, such as a lithe body with a fairly long tail to aid balance. But cats have evolved to suit their respective environments. Those that frequent the grasslands have developed long legs to enable them

---

COAT PATTERNING VARIES GREATLY IN THE LYNX AND OTHER SPECIES; ONE CAT MAY BE SPOTTED, ANOTHER PLAIN

---

to see over the tall grasses, while others have much shorter legs so that they can keep low to the ground as they creep up on their prey. Coat colors and patterns have also diversified to give cats a degree of camouflage in their surroundings. Markings vary from patterns of stripes and bars to blotches and spots and to virtually plain coloring. Most cats have big, soft-padded feet with five front toes, one of which does not touch the ground, and four rear toes. Each toe is equipped with a needle-sharp, hooked claw that is wholly or semiretractile.

Senses of hearing and vision are highly developed and acute across the species. Ear shapes and sizes vary to some extent, but the ears are always mobile so that they can be pricked to tune in to the slightest sound. Eyes are placed on the front of the face to give good binocular vision, important for pinpointing prey. It is said that cats have similar vision to humans in daylight, but the eye is constructed in a way that they are able to see six times better in the dark. The sense of smell is the least important in the lifestyle of cats and is thus the most poorly developed; it is used mainly in communication with one another rather than in locating prey.

Of all the cats considered here, the lynx is the largest. It can reach a head-and-body length of 51 in (130 cm) and a top weight of 64 lb (29 kg). The smallest of these small cats—indeed, one of the smallest of all wildcats—is the black-footed cat, which is roughly half the size of the average domestic cat. ∎

THE SMALL CATS' FAMILY TREE

The family tree shows the relationship between the big cats and the small cats of the world. The thirty species of small cats extend through North and South America and Africa, as well as through Europe and Asia. Some species, such as the lynx, occur on more than one continent. They all lead solitary and secretive lives and are closely related.

PALLAS'S CAT

Felis manul
(FEEL-iss man-OOL)

This distinctive-looking cat has an extensive range but is found only in isolated pockets across it. Besides its luxuriant coat, it may be distinguished by its short, thick legs; broad, somewhat blunted head; and short, rounded ears that are set low on the head and appear to be pushed backward. Some people believe this cat influenced long-haired domestic breeds, but this is very unlikely.

OTHER SPECIES:
ASIATIC GOLDEN CAT
CHINESE DESERT CAT
LEOPARD CAT
MARBLED CAT
BAY CAT
JUNGLE CAT
FLAT-HEADED CAT
FISHING CAT
IRIOMOTE CAT
RUSTY-SPOTTED CAT

NEW WORL
CATS

Color illustrations Peter David Scott/Wildlife Art Agency

EURASIAN WILDCAT

Felis silvestris
(FEEL-iss sil-VEST-ris)

Found over much of Europe, Africa, and western Asia, this cat, also known as the European wildcat, varies in size and markings across its range; in Scotland it resembles a large domestic tabby with a broad head and a short, thick, bushy tail that ends in a blunt tip. Because it breeds freely with feral domestic cats, intermediate forms also occur. Various subspecies, such as the African wildcat, F. s. lybica, and the Indian desert cat, F. s. ornata, are recognized.

LYNX

Felis lynx
(FEEL-iss links)

Usually regarded as the same species as that in North America, the Spanish lynx is thought by some to be a separate species, F. pardina. Basically a cat of cold climates and high altitudes, the Spanish lynx has adapted to warmer, lower areas in the southern parts of its European range. The northern lynxes have remarkably large feet, which are very densely furred; thus it is able to move easily over the snowy ground that characterizes much of its New World range.

B/W illustrations Ruth Grewcock

SMALL CATS

AFRICAN SMALL CATS

ALL CATS

ANATOMY:
THE EURASIAN WILDCAT

The Eurasian wildcat (above) is about one-third larger than the average domestic tabby cat. The smallest of all wildcats are the black-footed and rusty-spotted cats: They have a maximum head-and-body length of 19 in (48 cm) and a top weight of 6.6 lb (3 kg).

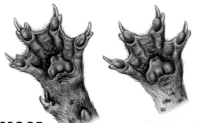

FOREFOOT   **HIND FOOT**

Like all small cats, the Eurasian wildcat (above) has five foreclaws and four hind claws; none of these claws leaves a print. The fishing cat (below) has partially webbed forefeet and its claws do not retract fully, so claw marks are visible in its footprints.

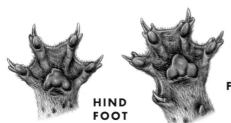

HIND FOOT   **FOREFOOT**

THE WHISKERS

are arranged in four rows and total twenty-four on each side of the face. Normally they extend at right angles to the jaws to detect air currents and give a cat information about objects on either side. When hunting, they tend to be brought forward into a "net," pointing more in the direction of the mouth, where they help the cat position a fatal bite to prey. In a defensive posture, a cat usually angles the whiskers back to lie more alongside its face.

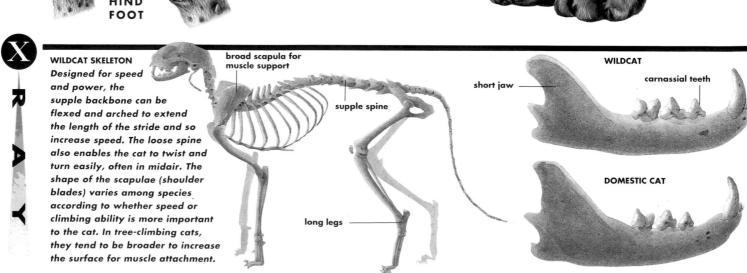

X

X-RAY

WILDCAT SKELETON
Designed for speed and power, the supple backbone can be flexed and arched to extend the length of the stride and so increase speed. The loose spine also enables the cat to twist and turn easily, often in midair. The shape of the scapulae (shoulder blades) varies among species according to whether speed or climbing ability is more important to the cat. In tree-climbing cats, they tend to be broader to increase the surface for muscle attachment.

broad scapula for muscle support

supple spine

long legs

WILDCAT

short jaw

carnassial teeth

DOMESTIC CAT

X-ray illustrations Elisabeth Smith

FACIAL EXPRESSION

When staring at prey, a cat pricks its ears forward and narrows its pupils (above left). Ears pricked and turned out (above center) denote aggression, while depressed ears and dilated pupils (above right) signify defensive submission.

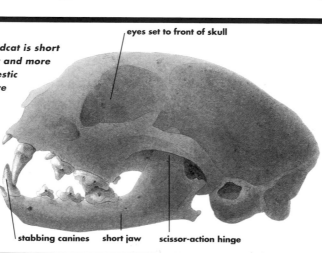

THE COAT

bears tabbylike markings. The body stripes are complete but usually indistinct. Stripes from the head and nape merge into a single line along the spine. The upperparts are a dark gray-brown, while the undersides are paler and may be spotted. White markings occur on the throat and often between the hind legs.

FACT FILE:

EURASIAN WILDCAT

CLASSIFICATION

GENUS: *FELIS*
SPECIES: *SILVESTRIS*

SIZE

HEAD–BODY LENGTH: 19.5–29 IN (50–75 CM)
TAIL LENGTH: 8–14 IN (21–36 CM)
WEIGHT: 6.5–17.5 LB (3–8 KG)
SIZE VARIES ACCORDING TO LOCATION; MALES ARE LARGER THAN FEMALES
WEIGHT AT BIRTH: 1.4 OZ (40 G)

COLORATION

VARIES ACROSS RANGE: USUALLY A GRAY-BROWN BASE COLOR WITH INDISTINCT BUT COMPLETE STRIPES AROUND THE BODY; UNDERPARTS ARE PALER AND THERE IS A WHITE CHEST MARK LONGITUDINAL STRIPES OVER FACE MERGE AT BASE OF NECK INTO A DORSAL STRIPE THAT EXTENDS TO, BUT NOT ALONG, THE TAIL

FEATURES

EARS RESEMBLE THOSE OF THE DOMESTIC TABBY IN THEIR SHAPE AND SIZE RELATIVE TO THE BODY
TAIL IS SHORT AND THICK WITH BLUNT, BLACK TIP AND DARK RINGS
LEGS ARE LONGER THAN THOSE OF THE DOMESTIC CAT

THE TAIL

is thicker and shorter than that of a domestic cat, with a blunt, black tip. Three to five complete rings encircle the lower part, and the hair is thick and long.

WILDCAT SKULL

The skull of the Eurasian wildcat is short and rounded, but it is larger and more robust than that of the domestic cat. The large eye sockets are positioned toward the front of the skull, reflecting the importance of vision and good distance judgment in cats. The jaws are scissor-hinged so that they move in one plane only; cats can deliver a very powerful bite but cannot chew effectively.

eyes set to front of skull

stabbing canines   short jaw   scissor-action hinge

The wildcat's braincase is larger and more robust than that of a domestic cat, with a volume of more than 2 cu in, as compared with around 1.95 cu in for the latter. Another aid to recognition lies in the the suture (joint) along the top of the crown, which in the wildcat is more convoluted.

large cranium (braincase)

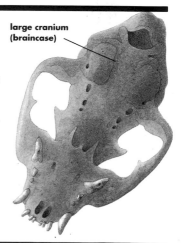

SOLITARY STALKERS

MOST CATS—BIG OR SMALL—LEAD LIVES THAT FOLLOW SIMILAR PATTERNS. SOLITARY AND OFTEN AT THEIR MOST ACTIVE AT NIGHT, MUCH OF THEIR TIME IS SPENT SILENTLY HUNTING PREY

Of all wildcats, it is really only the lion that has evolved any social lifestyle. Individuals in most other species seek each other out only for breeding, and the only bonds that form are those between a female and her kittens. Even these bonds rarely last longer than a few months. Interestingly, however, the feral descendants of domestic cats that have gone wild often associate together, particularly around an area where food is abundant. In such instances they may form a loose but clearly defined hierarchy under a dominant male, and they may even help care for each other's young.

By and large, small cats are seldom seen or heard. This is due in part to size: The smaller the cat, the more vulnerable it is and the more likely it is to be taken by larger carnivores—even by other cats. This partly explains the small cats' furtive streak, and to some extent accounts for their nocturnal habits. However, they are often active by night simply because this is when most of their prey victims are also out and about. Small cats need to be more active than their larger relatives: Where a large cat will often take an animal bigger than itself to satisfy its hunger for a few days, small cats often hunt mouse-sized prey and may need to make several kills a night.

CAT CALLS

Small cats cannot roar in the manner of big cats. The voice box of a big cat is attached to a ligament that vibrates to magnify the sound; small cats lack this flexibility. Most small cats, however, can voice at least six distinctive calls, four of which may act as a warning either of their presence or of their aggression. In addition, females have special calls to attract the attention of their young when necessary, and all small cats can purr—something big cats cannot do. Purring is usually taken as a sign of contentment, but it may also signify anxiety.

In some parts of their range, many of the small cats happen to live fairly close to one another, so they have evolved ways of detecting others in order to avoid them when possible. They achieve this mainly through scent marking—except in actual confrontation, where calling comes into play. Inevitably there are times when cats come across one another, and, for such occasions, they have evolved a complex and comprehensive set of body signals to communicate mood and intent.

It may seem a little strange that animals that lead such solitary lives should have such elaborate communication methods. Aggression is clearly signaled when an encounter takes place; it begins with an unwavering stare, one cat fixing the other with narrowed eyes. Further displays may involve raising

They may lack stamina, but small cats—like this rusty-spotted cat (above)—*are superb pouncers.*

Reinhard Siegal/Aquila

Terry Whittaker/Frank Lane Picture Agency

FELINE LORE

Across their range and across the centuries, cats have been revered and valued. Ancient Egyptians worshiped cats and even mummified them after death; and almost every country has a stock of stories and legends surrounding them.

In the British Isles, a prince of South Wales set a value on cats that he laid down in laws. A newborn kitten was worth one penny. From the time its eyes opened until it could kill mice it was worth two cents. Thereafter its worth was measured by its weight in corn. These prices dictated the penalty that had to be paid for killing one.

In Thailand the Asiatic golden cat still has a special worth. It is known as the fire tiger, and it is believed that by burning its fur, tigers will be kept away. In some villages, these cats are cooked, fur and all; locals believe that eating them gives protection from all wild animals.

the fur on the body so as to appear bigger; showing teeth while hissing, snarling, and spitting; and finally lashing out with a pawful of unsheathed claws. The idea of such a display is to try to avoid an actual fight whenever possible. All cats are superbly equipped to kill, having to do so in order to feed. If they turn their teeth and claws on one another, they could inflict serious injury or even death and risk damage to their own tools of the hunting trade.

CATS VERSUS DOGS

Few cats hunt their prey by chasing it over open country in the manner of a dog pack, for example. They have sacrificed speed and stamina for a more self-contained power in their limbs, and they will make only a short sprint before pouncing. Unlike dogs, cats are short-winded—they have relatively small hearts in comparison to other animals—which may account for their lack of endurance. However, also unlike dogs, many cats can climb well and will hunt prey in trees, as well as taking to the branches for safety when danger threatens. Although some of the small cats discussed here are forest-dwellers, few are truly arboreal. And, contrary to the apparent reticence of most domestic cats, cats in the wild are generally good swimmers, taking to water quite happily whenever necessary. ■

The ears of most lynx are adorned with long black tufts, which serve as mood indicators.

HABITATS

The Eurasian wildcat has the widest distribution of any of the small cats. Although not common anywhere, it ranges from Scotland to central India—where it occurs as the Indian desert cat—and China. In the United Kingdom it is now confined to Scotland, but in the Mediterranean it is found on a number of islands including Sardinia, Corsica, and Crete.

The wildcat's chosen habitat varies according to location. In Scotland it seeks sheltered heath and woodland, usually at altitudes below 1,650 ft (500 m); in other places it is found in more open habitats, but it always needs some shelter, such as rocks or scrub thickets. In Europe it lives up to altitudes of 6,560 ft (2,000 m). Most active at dawn and dusk, it often rests by day in a hollow tree or rock crevice. As an active climber, however, it may choose to sun itself high up in a tree, draped along a branch. One wildcat was spotted resting in a large bird's nest!

Outside of Scotland, the Eurasian wildcat likes to live in warm, dry areas whenever possible, although it has adapted to damp and cool conditions when necessary. Its existence in Scotland is explained by the comparatively mild climate brought by the Gulf Stream to the far north. It is none too happy in long, cold winters or areas of deep snow.

Hellio & van Ingen

THE LYNX

The lynx is the only small cat that occurs in both Eurasia and the Americas. It first evolved as the Issoir lynx in Africa between three and four million years ago, at which time it was a little larger—certainly taller—than its current forms. Fossil records have been found in Europe, where it probably gave rise to the Spanish lynx—often still considered to be a separate species—and in China, where it evolved into the Eurasian lynx. Finally it crossed the land bridge from Asia into North America, where it continued to thrive and finally developed into the North American lynx. Although these three animals are normally referred to as a single species, the lynx that occurs in Spain weighs only half as much as other lynxes, and it is also generally more heavily spotted. Similarly, the Eurasian lynx is about twice the size of its North American counterpart and usually has a more pronounced pattern of spots.

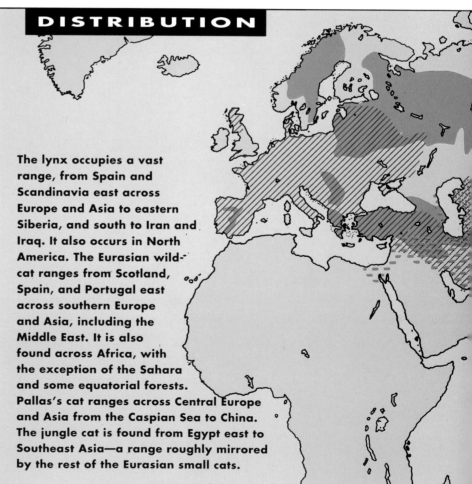

DISTRIBUTION

The lynx occupies a vast range, from Spain and Scandinavia east across Europe and Asia to eastern Siberia, and south to Iran and Iraq. It also occurs in North America. The Eurasian wildcat ranges from Scotland, Spain, and Portugal east across southern Europe and Asia, including the Middle East. It is also found across Africa, with the exception of the Sahara and some equatorial forests. Pallas's cat ranges across Central Europe and Asia from the Caspian Sea to China. The jungle cat is found from Egypt east to Southeast Asia—a range roughly mirrored by the rest of the Eurasian small cats.

The lynx's fragmented range stretches across western Europe, from the Iberian Peninsula and southern France across to Turkey, and east to Kashmir and Tibet. Farther north it extends to eastern Siberia. At one time the lynx also lived on the island of Sardinia. It favors woodlands of any altitude, especially forests with dense undergrowth. But it is above all adaptable, so it also ventures into more open woodland and rocky ground. In its New World range, it is also found on the more barren tundra. Active mainly after sundown, it spends the day resting under rocky ledges or fallen trees.

RAIN FOREST AND DESERT

A cat of hotter climates, the Asiatic golden cat is also often found in woodland—both deciduous and tropical rain forest—yet spends most of its life on the ground, despite its skills at climbing. In some areas it is found in more open country, such as brushland with rocky outcrops. Its range extends from Tibet and Nepal to southeastern China and the Malaysian Peninsula. It is also found on the island of Sumatra.

There are three widely distributed races of lynx: the Eurasian (left), Spanish, and North American.

A jungle cat scouts out the undergrowth of an Indian national park in search of prey (above).

The thick coat of Pallas's cat reflects its more northerly habitat; it ranges eastward from Iran and the Caspian Sea to western and central China. The arid, inhospitable deserts and steppes of the Altai Mountains, parts of Mongolia, and Kazakhstan are within its domain, and it has been found on rocky plateaus at altitudes of 13,125 ft (4,000 m). Often the ground is either icy or snowbound, which explains the dense belly fur on Pallas's cat. Found in more open habitats than many of its cousins, its plain coat provides it with superb camouflage. Pallas's cat usually hunts at night, sleeping by day in caves, rocky niches, or abandoned burrows of other animals.

The habitat of the Chinese desert cat belies its name, for it is found most frequently on steppes or scrub-covered mountainsides. The soles of its feet are protected by long hair growing between the toes—an indication of temperature extremes, usually either burning sand or freezing snow. This species is native to central Asia, including southern Mongolia and western China.

SOUTHERN ASIAN CATS

The jungle cat is true to its name and occurs in humid forests, but its range covers such a wide area that it has also adapted to other habitats: mixed woodlands, open terrain, and even reedbeds. From

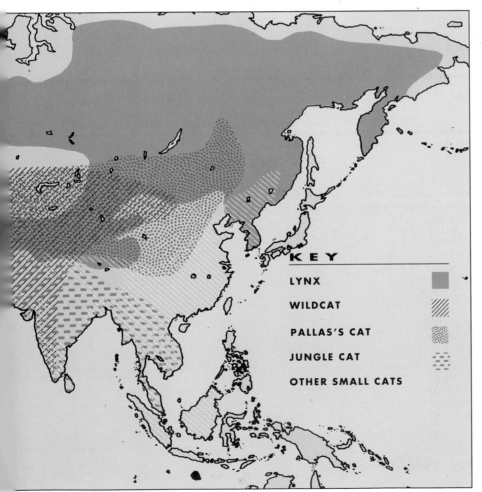

KEY

LYNX

WILDCAT

PALLAS'S CAT

JUNGLE CAT

OTHER SMALL CATS

here it spreads east through the Middle East, Nepal, Burma, and Malaysia to southwestern China; it is also found in Sri Lanka. Across its range it occurs from sea level to elevations of 7,875 ft (2,400 m). An occasional neighbor is the rusty-spotted cat, which is found mainly in southern India and Sri Lanka. In India it occurs in open and scrub country, but in Sri Lanka it prefers the humid mountain forests.

The fishing cat is one of the few cats that really relish a watery habitat. Occurring in Sri Lanka, a few areas in India, and through Malaysia, Sumatra, and Java, it is found in marshes, reedbeds, mangroves, and the thick vegetation along creeks and rivers. In the Himalayas it occurs as high as 4,920 ft (1,500 m). The flat-headed cat is also often found near water in forest and scrub. Its homeland includes Thailand, Malaysia, Borneo, and Sumatra.

The leopard cat shares its home with the flat-headed cat, but extends farther both north and west to Burma, mainland China, Pakistan, India, and Bangladesh. It is also found on Borneo and in the Philippines and Taiwan. Being a good swimmer, it has colonized a number of outlying islands. Mainly a forest-dweller that likes water, it inhabits a variety of wooded areas across its range, from taiga forest to tropical forest, and is at home from sea level up to 9,840 ft (3,000 m). The marbled cat is found in a

Manfred Danegger/NHPA

FOCUS ON

NORTHERN SCOTLAND

Widely inhabited in prehistoric times, northern Scotland is now one of the least inhabited areas of the British Isles: 98 percent of Scotland is classified as countryside. The northeast is deeply penetrated by the North Sea, and there are numerous islands dotted around the coastline.

Scotland may be divided into three principal areas: the Southern Uplands, the Central Lowlands, and the Highlands. The Highlands includes the northeastern area, which is dominated by the Grampian Mountains. The Great Glen Fault, that stretches from Loch Linnhe to the Moray Firth, is a natural divide between the Grampians and the northwest Highlands.

Although the Highlands are low by alpine standards, much of the area lies above 2,000 ft (610 m). In fact, the wildcat is seldom seen above 1,640 ft (500 m) in this part of the world, although it inhabits higher altitudes in Europe. The Highlands were once a haven for wildlife, home to such species as the reindeer, brown bear, and wild boar—all now extinct in this area. However, it is still home to the red deer and several birds of prey.

TEMPERATURE AND RAINFALL

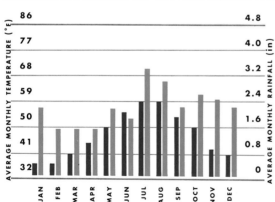

■ **TEMPERATURE**

■ **RAINFALL**

Northern Scotland is notoriously wet and windy, with high rainfall in summer. Although the winters can be bitterly cold, the temperature is sustained by the Gulf Stream, a warm ocean current that crosses the Atlantic to Europe from the Gulf of Mexico.

narrow band from northern India and Nepal east to Burma, Thailand, and Malaysia, as well as Borneo and Sumatra. It is strictly a forest-dweller and is more arboreal than most other small cats.

On their island homes of Borneo and Iriomote respectively, the bay cat and Iriomote cat are both found in forests. The bay cat inhabits areas on the edge of the forest and jungle, while the Iriomote cat is found in tropical jungles. There are only about forty Iriomote cats in the wild, on an island with an area of 108 square miles (280 square kilometers). ■

NEIGHBORS

Like the wildcat itself, many of its neighbors in Scotland were once far more widespread across Great Britain. In most cases, their decline in range is the result of persecution by mankind.

SPARROW HAWK

Common over a wide area, this bird of prey flies low over the ground in search of small birds and rodents.

TOAD

This toad hibernates all through the winter, waking to find a breeding pond in March or early April.

ENEMIES

WEASEL
The fierce little weasel may prey on a wildcat's kittens, but an adult cat is more than a match for it.

SCOTLAND
In northern Scotland the wildcat ranges from Campbeltown in Kintyre on the west coast and north through the Grampians and Highlands as far as John o' Groats. It is absent from many of the Western Isles and from low-lying eastern coastal areas.

WILDCAT DISTRIBUTION

PINE MARTEN

Rare and elusive, the pine marten is about the size of a cat, with a bushy tail similar to a fox's brush.

HOODED CROW

A subspecies of the carrion crow, this bird differs from its more familiar relative in having gray plumage.

RED DEER

Largest of Britain's native land mammals, the red deer is fairly common in its Scottish stronghold.

OTTER

The streamlined otter, once common throughout Britain, is now mainly confined to Scotland.

RED SQUIRREL

Declining woodland and competition from the gray squirrel has forced the red squirrel into remote areas.

HUNTING

Ferrero/Labat/Ardea

Of all the carnivores, cats are the best equipped as hunter-killers, and meat forms their staple diet. This applies every bit as much to the smallest of the wildcats as it does to the lion. Everything about a cat's anatomy supports this lifestyle. The long, curved, and needle-sharp canine teeth are ideal for seizing prey and piercing flesh. Large, purposeful carnassials slice and tear off flesh to be swallowed in chunks—hence the absence of real grinding molars at the back of the jaw. The tongue has a rough surface that is ideal for rasping the fur off the belly to get to the organs.

All cats track their prey with their acute eyesight and hearing, and in some species these senses are quite superb. The lynx and the jungle cat, both of which often hunt in tall grass or dense undergrowth, have ears that act like antennae and help them pick up the faintest of sounds. Cats hunt most of their prey by stealth, creeping closer on their big, soft paws and freezing if the prey shows any sign of alarm. Their final act is a pounce, preferably without a last-minute chase. If a prey victim escapes, a cat will very rarely be able to outrun it and, indeed, seldom tries.

SLASH AND GRAB

As a cat pounces or lashes out at a prey victim with a paw, its claws slip out of their sheaths and dig like meat hooks into the prey to hold it firm. When pouncing on a small, stationary animal, the cat uses both paws. Whereas big cats may kill large prey through suffocation, by holding the throat in a vice-like grip between the teeth, small cats nearly always kill with a deadly accurate bite to the spinal cord, crunching their incisors down deep between the vertebrae. Very occasionally, they may shake the animal repeatedly as they bite it until it is dead.

Some cats lie in wait for prey—perhaps by a burrow or beside a well-worn path—and ambush it as it passes, grabbing or pouncing on it in the usual way. The fishing cat sits patiently on a rock or sandbank in a stream, ever ready to hook a passing fish out of the water. This may be why its claws are never fully retracted. This cat also wades in the shallows for fish, and it has even been known to dive after a fish, seizing it in its mouth like an otter. It also eats water snails, frogs, and crustaceans, while on land it takes birds, small mammals, and snakes. Its heavy

The stocky, powerful lynx sometimes tackles large prey such as deer (above), but it usually eats rabbits and hares.

PRICKLY PREY

The jungle cat eats anything from frogs and lizards to chital fawns, but it may try its luck with tougher prey. The porcupine (left), which is attacked also by leopards and lions, is armed with sharp quills that can maim or even kill an enemy if they are left to fester in the flesh.

KILLER ALOFT

The rusty-spotted cat of India and Sri Lanka (right) is a skillful climber, finding much of its prey in the trees. It catches birds and small mammals, as well as insects, frogs, and reptiles.

reliance on aquatic prey allows it to coexist with other cats, such as the Asiatic golden cat, which prefers to hunt on dry land. Another cat that includes fish in its diet is the flat-headed cat, whose teeth and claws are well suited to seizing slippery prey.

Big cats have the strength and ability to kill animals as big as or bigger than themselves, whereas most small cats rely on small prey. The European wildcat, which generally hunts along a well-known system of trails, stalks or ambushes its prey as described, but often ends the hunt with a short, sharp chase. It usually kills its prey on the spot, but occasionally it carries it away to store for later. Birds, rabbits, hares, and small rodents are the

mainstays of its diet, but it will eat reptiles and insects when times are lean. In parts of France, the dormouse sustains wildcats in the autumn; most of these cats feed heavily at this time of year, putting on a layer of fat to help them survive the winter.

Some of the larger small cats, such as the Asiatic golden cat, can hunt correspondingly larger animals, such as small deer. The leopard cat eats cave-living bats and fish, as well as hares, rodents, reptiles, and birds. Jungle cats prey on the fawns of local spotted deer and also take porcupines. These long-legged cats are capable of remarkable bursts of speed of up to 20 mph (32 km/h). They can also leap high into the air to swipe at low-flying birds. ∎

FISHHOOKS

Sleek, spotted, and powerfully built, the fishing cat regularly puts its swimming skills into practice, actively chasing fish through the water. More usually it stands in the shallows, ready to hook its prey from the water (right).

in SIGHT
LEARNING TO HUNT

Cats are good hunters by instinct, but a young orphaned cat is less likely to survive if its mother has not provided it with learning opportunities. Some of the actions are innate: Kittens will swipe at, or pounce on, anything that moves; but these actions must be turned into effective predatory skills. A mother cat teaches her kittens by first bringing them small animals she has killed. Because she presents prey to the kittens whole, they must first learn how to tear it apart with their teeth. Next, she brings live prey and stands by as the kittens try to catch it; she repeatedly recaptures the victim as it escapes their clutches. Once having trapped the prey, they must learn how to kill it.

Illustrations R. Carter/Wildlife Art Agency

TERRITORY

Small, solitary animals such as cats have had to evolve a system of living peaceably at close quarters with others of the same species—together and yet apart. The most important thing is to let others know of their presence, so that whenever possible they may avoid one another.

Most wildcats live within a recognized and marked territory, the size of which depends on the type of environment and the availability of prey within it. Where prey is plentiful and there is lots of shelter, a territory might be pretty small. If the countryside is more open, both predator and prey may have to wander over a considerably larger area. Wildcats in Scotland, for example, live in territories of some 124 acres (50 hectares) in woodland; when their home is the open moorland, this area

> DOMESTIC TOMCATS DEFEND BACKYARD
> TERRITORIES IN MUCH THE SAME WAY
> AS THEIR WILD COUNTERPARTS

can be four times the size. Lynx home ranges may be 4–116 square miles (11–300 square kilometers). Within its restricted island environment, the Iriomote cat's home range is no more than 0.75 square miles (2 square kilometers). The home range of a male often overlaps with those of females, but it is unlikely to overlap with that of another male. If food is scarce locally, or if there are no females, males may wander farther afield.

SCRATCH AND SNIFF

Cats mark their territories in a number of ways to advertise their presence and, in the case of females, their breeding condition. Many of the *Felis* species have scent glands on the rump, footpads, chin, and cheeks. When a cat rubs its head against a tree trunk or stretches up to scratch the bark, it will leave behind secretions, as well as the scratches, for other cats to detect. Scratching is also a good way of conditioning the claws. As it rubs its head on a territorial marker, a cat usually also produces a lot of saliva. This is spread around by the rubbing action, both on the marker and on the cat's face, leaving a scent message for others to detect. Urine is the main secretion used in marking a territory (see box). Most small cats do not leave feces as other animals do; instead, they usually bury them. Nor are secretions of the anal gland mixed with the urine when marking. In this regard, the function of the anal glands of cats remains somewhat unclear.

The leopard cat (right) *lives in a wide range of habitats over Asia. Like all cats, it is solitary and rarely tolerates other cats within its territory.*

ROLL-ON SCENT

A marbled cat rubs its facial scent glands upon a territorial marker flag—a stone, stump, or twig—to delineate the bounds of its domain (below).

Around their territories, wildcats will have a number of dens or sheltered resting spots where they mainly spend their days. Wildcats in Scotland choose places that give them a good view over their immediate surroundings—perhaps a hollow in a pile of rocks or under a fallen tree. Occasionally they may shelter in an abandoned fox earth. Most wildcats look for and establish dens in similar places—caves, old tree trunks, abandoned burrows of animals they share their environment with, or dense undergrowth.

In spite of all the precautions taken to avoid one another, encounters between wildcats of the same species are inevitable. A cat whose territory has been invaded is

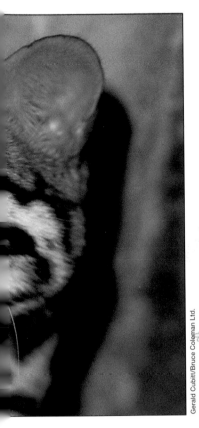

BAY SPRAY

The bay cat of Borneo lives in forests, from the deepest thickets to the rocky fringes, and marks its range by spraying copiously (right).

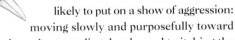

likely to put on a show of aggression: moving slowly and purposefully toward the intruder, growling deeply, and twitching the end of its tail in warning. It may raise the fur on its body to increase the impression of size. The aggressive posture is intended to scare off the intruder without having to engage in actual conflict. The intruder, on the other hand, will often respond by crouching with every muscle tensed; it will look around while deliberately avoiding the stare of the other cat.

If the intruder does not slink off, physical conflict is likely to follow. The intruder prepares to roll over on its back, which allows it to strike out with its forepaws at the nose and vulnerable underparts of the aggressor. Often the two cats roll around on the ground locked in combat, attempting to bite and scratch at one another, while yowling and hissing at the same time.

An encounter in which a wildcat is confronted by a possible predator takes a slightly different form. Here the intention is definitely not to engage in physical conflict, but instead to startle the intruder so that it stops in its tracks, giving the cat time to flee to safety. ∎

SPRAYING

All cats mark their territories by urinating, although it is the males that do so most persistently. The position of the male's penis enables it to spray backward between its hind limbs, in the same way as a domestic male cat will spray when it enters another's yard, for example.

This marking is almost ritualistic. A cat first sniffs intently at a spot to be marked, possibly to detect a previous marking. It then turns around and backs up to the site, sprays it, and turns around to sniff again. It may then rub its head against the sprayed object, thereby also impregnating itself with the scent.

Females also mark with urine, but they tend to do this most frequently when advertising for a mate. In general, however, scent is less important to cats than it is to other carnivores—cats rely primarily upon visual and vocal communication.

LIFE CYCLE

When breeding time comes, it is usually the female of wildcat species that advertises her receptivity by calling in a particular way and indulging in scent marking—rubbing against the ground and various objects. In this way she soon attracts the attention of a male. Sexual encounters are markedly friendly. As the male approaches, the female may roll over on the ground in a submissive manner. She may also rub against him, and the two rub necks together. Vocalizations during courtship and mating are gentle and inviting—usually soft meows and loud purring.

SEASONAL BREEDING

Breeding among most small cats occurs once a year, although second or even third litters may occur in temperate areas. The European wildcat in Scotland, for example, mates mainly in March; in other parts of Europe and Asia mating may occur anytime from January to March. Asiatic golden cat kittens are born in February. Lynx in Spain mate mainly in January, while leopard cats in Siberia generally mate in the spring. In most species, if a female loses a litter for any reason, she is likely to come into estrus again and will resume the search for a mate.

INVITATION

Living alone, the female wildcat must make an effort to attract a mate. She does this by calling (right) and by leaving sexual clues in her scent deposits.

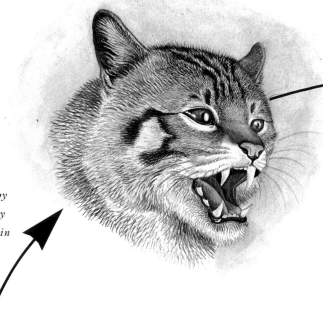

LESSONS IN HUNTING

The young gain hunting skills when their mother brings them live prey for practice (right).

Gestation periods and litter sizes vary. The European wildcat typically has two to four kittens about sixty-six days after mating. For the lynx, gestation may be a few days longer, and there can be up to five kittens in a litter—although in Spain two or three is more common. For Pallas's cat, litter size is generally five or six. Jungle cats are thought to produce two litters a year in some parts of their range, and there may be as many as seven in a litter. Gestation in these cats is about eight weeks.

Although in most instances a male cat has nothing more to do with the female after mating, it may assist in raising the young in some species; for example, in the leopard cat. Male fishing cats have been known to help care for the young in captivity, but it is uncertain whether they also do so in the wild. The

Although their weapons are pin-sharp from the start, they need protection for several months (left).

GROWING UP

The life of a young wildcat

SECRET BIRTH

The female prepares a special nursery den where her young will be protected from predators. She licks the afterbirth from the newborns as they are born (left).

FEEDING

The tiny, sightless kittens can do little except suckle. They knead the female's abdomen (above) *to stimulate the flow of milk—a habit that is displayed even by mature domestic cats when they find a soft rug or sweater.*

European wildcat may be monogamous on occasion—the same pair breed year after year, even if they do not spend their entire lives together. The male may bring food to the den after the female has given birth, although the female is likely to chase him off if he comes too close to her kittens.

All kittens are born blind, deaf, and helpless—unable to walk or do anything except suckle. Their one action is to knead their feet against the mother's body close to a teat to stimulate the flow of milk. Births always occur in a sheltered den established in advance by the female: possibly an old burrow, in a hollow under some rocks, or deep within dense vegetation. Kittens are fully furred, some in a similar pattern to adults, others showing different markings. Those of the jungle cat, whose adult coat shows very little in the way of markings, are born with distinctive tabby patterning, which may help camouflage them;

they are usually born in reedbeds. Pallas's cat kittens have thick, woolly coats at birth, but the white tips that give the frosted appearance in adult cats do not appear until later.

DEFENSIVE MOTHERS

A female is ferocious in defense of her young. At first she spend most of her time in the den with the kittens, feeding and cleaning them. By licking them she encourages them to excrete waste matter, which she consumes; this helps to prevent predators from sniffing out the hiding place. Most kittens open their eyes when they are about ten days old, but they rarely make their first foray outside the den until they are a month or so old. Then they begin to play with one another, chasing and mock-fighting while the mother goes hunting. If, on her return, she finds they have strayed too far from the den for her liking, she either calls them to her or gently carries them back to the den in her jaws.

European wildcat kittens are fully weaned at about four months. Also around this time they start to climb and the mother begins teaching them to hunt. She may start by lying close and twitching her tail to attract them, encouraging them to jump on it and pin it to the ground with their paws.

At two to three months old, the kittens have learned enough to accompany the mother on hunting trips to improve their skills. At around five months old, each young cat disperses to establish its own territory. At this time the adolescents are easy prey for predators, including larger adult male cats, but their births have usually been timed to ensure that other prey is abundant. In temperate areas, by the time the winter comes, the young cats have established their home ranges and honed their hunting skills, so they are better able to survive the harsher conditions. In most species they will be ready to breed themselves the following year; the lynx, however, does not reach sexual maturity until nearly two years old in females and a year later in males. ∎

FROM BIRTH TO DEATH

EUROPEAN WILDCAT	LYNX
GESTATION: AVERAGE 66 DAYS	**GESTATION:** 9–10 WEEKS
LITTER SIZE: 2–4	**LITTER SIZE:** UP TO 5, USUALLY 2–3
WEIGHT AT BIRTH: 1.4 oz (40 G)	IN SPANISH SPECIES
EYES OPEN: 10 DAYS	**WEIGHT AT BIRTH:** 7 oz (200 G)
WEANED: FROM 7 WEEKS; FULLY	**EYES OPEN:** NOT KNOWN
AT 4 MONTHS	**WEANED:** 5 MONTHS
INDEPENDENCE: 5 MONTHS	**INDEPENDENCE:** 8 MONTHS
FULLY GROWN: 10 MONTHS	**SEXUAL MATURITY:** MALES 33
SEXUAL MATURITY: 1 YEAR	MONTHS, FEMALES 21 MONTHS
LONGEVITY: 15 YEARS IN	**LONGEVITY:** 26 YEARS IN
CAPTIVITY	CAPTIVITY

Illustrations Robin Budden/Wildlife Art Agency

Too Small To Notice

THE PLIGHT OF MANY SMALL CATS IS EVERY BIT AS DESPERATE AS THAT OF THEIR LARGER RELATIVES. WITH THEIR SMALLER SIZE, HOWEVER, THEY HAVE FAILED TO ATTRACT THE SAME ATTENTION

S mall cats have never had the same appeal as their larger relatives or been noticed in the same way. In one regard, this has worked in their favor: Their smaller size, secretive lifestyle, and resulting lower profile means they have not appealed to the bloodlust of the big-game hunters as much as the big cats.

However, various factors have led to a decrease in numbers of nearly all small cat species over the years, and as they have become increasingly more scarce, they have largely failed to capture the imagination of conservationists, let alone the general public. "Save the European wildcat" does not have the same universal appeal as "save the tiger." Nor will such campaigns have the same advantages in terms of the tourist trade, for few people are going to venture in search of the elusive European wildcat in its natural habitat. Meanwhile their small size has actually not released these cats from the pressure of hunting. Over the years, like their larger relatives, they have been killed for three main reasons: for sport, because they have been considered pests, and for their fur.

HUNTING AND PERSECUTION

Today, hunting wild animals for sport is probably less of a threat to just about all species than it had been for many years. Such activity is mainly controlled by law, a defined number of animals being allowed to be shot only if it is necessary to cull that species. In the 1960s, for example, the Spanish authorities allowed twenty lynx to be killed legally each year within the Coto Doñana National Park. Now its numbers are too critical to permit even this.

European wildcats in Britain have a long history of persecution because of their reputation as pests. Gamekeepers north and south of the Scottish border considered wildcats as vermin and killed them indiscriminately. Farmers did the same, claiming the

wildcats preyed heavily upon newborn lambs. By the early 1850s, the European wildcat had disappeared from south of the Trent River and twenty-five years later it was virtually unknown south of Scotland's Great Flen Fault.

The wildcat is a resilient species, however, and has very few natural predators in the wild. Largely left alone by humans during World War I, it was able to reestablish itself to some extent in Scotland. By the end of World War II, it was known to have returned to Argyll, Perth, and west Aberdeenshire. More recently, it is thought to have recolonized the Border area and may even have stretched farther south into Cumbria. By the 1980s gamekeepers were once more killing these cats whenever they

Too little is known about the rusty-spotted cat
(above) *to ascertain its rarity status.*

Reinhard Siegal/Aquila

This map shows the current distribution of the bay cat on the island of Borneo, Southeast Asia.

■ CURRENT DISTRIBUTION

The bay cat of Borneo is one of the most elusive of all wildcats. It has been reported in only a few sites on the island and is known mainly from museum specimens as much as one hundred years old. There are no accounts of sightings in the wild. Like all of Borneo's wildlife, the bay cat is steadily losing its habitat. The northern populations in the states of Sabah and Sarawak are especially threatened by logging activities, cultivation, and shortages of prey.

could, particularly on grouse moors. Several hundred were killed annually, in spite of the fact that they were still uncommon. Wildcats were finally given full legal protection in 1988, but it is unlikely that the killing has entirely ceased. Gamekeepers are still concerned about their grouse, and there is evidence that a number are killed each year during legally organized hunts to control the fox population.

THE FUR TRADE

For some time, the small cats escaped the worst ravages of the fur trade, possibly because it takes so many more pelts to make a coat. For example, a coat of leopard cat fur requires about fifteen pelts. As the plight of the world's large cats gained public notoriety, however, and as they were given increasing

The anti–fur trade organization Lynx took its name from this widespread but rare felid.

1271

ENDANGERED SPECIES

protection, the attentions of the fur traders have turned to some of the smaller cats.

Small cat pelts are no less luxuriant and beautifully marked than those of the tiger or leopard. The Asian golden cat, the lynx, the leopard cat, Pallas's cat, the Chinese desert cat (particularly when it grows its thick winter coat), the fishing cat, and the marbled cat have all been singled out by the fur traders. At the end of the 1980s, it was claimed that at least 2,000 skins of Pallas's cat went to the international fur trade each year, while some two million leopard cats were killed between 1985 and 1988 in China alone. Exports of skins to Europe were prohibited in 1987, but there is still a market in other places. Trade in leopard cat skins has a sad irony: Until comparatively recently they had little commercial value because for some reason they did not wear well. Technology came to the "rescue" in the form of a special chemical that, when applied to the fur, renders it more durable. The leopard cat itself does not help its situation—this is one of the few wildcats that seems to be relatively at home around people, and it is often found near villages, making hunting and trapping it comparatively easy.

THE NUMBER OF ALL ANIMAL FURS
CURRENTLY IN TRADE IS BELIEVED
TO BE AROUND FIFTEEN MILLION

The controlling body of trade in wild animals and their parts is CITES (The Convention on International Trade in Endangered Species of Wild Flora and Fauna). CITES has put a ban on international trade in the pelts of certain species, but the only small cat to receive full protection is the marbled cat. The leopard cat, for example, is protected only in certain parts of its range. Trade is still legal in other species; it is supposed to be controlled under the Convention, but enforcing restrictions is impossible in the more remote habitats. The only effective way of stopping trade is to kill the demand for fur coats. Although this fashion has lost popularity in recent decades, there are still some people who will pay vast sums of money for such an item, thereby sustaining the trade. In May 1994, for example, wildlife officials seized a total of 2,133 skins from a train depot in Jammu and Kashmir, India; these included one thousand jungle cat and eight fishing cat pelts, as well as foxes, jackals, and civets.

HABITAT LOSS

The other great factor that affects the future of so many animals in the wild is the destruction of their habitat. Forests of all types all over the world continue to be destroyed at a terrifying rate. Grasslands

I. Ledgerwood/Natural Science Photos

THE LYNX

The lynx, with its attractive coat and handsome head, has long been appreciated by humans. In Norse mythology the animal was associated with Freya, the goddess of love and beauty. Like most cats, it has also been sought after for its fur and has suffered accordingly across its range.

Hunting a solitary cat in deep forest is hard work, so many trappers use the banned gin or leghold trap instead. This device has a pair of spring-loaded jaws activated by a pressure pad; the jaws slam shut on an animal's leg with such force that the bones are often snapped and the flesh deeply cut. These traps will ensnare any animals that stray onto them, such as large birds or domestic pets. One trapped lynx in Alaska clung to life for six weeks because its siblings brought food to it.

Across its Eurasian range, the lynx has suffered a decline for most of the reasons already discussed. The Spanish lynx has been affected by one of its main prey animals, rabbits, in two ways. First, several lynx have been caught in traps set for rabbits, and second, a recent epidemic of myxomatosis among rabbits had a disastrous domino effect. Deprived of rabbits, lynx roamed farther afield to find prey, bringing them into direct competition with foxes, which are far more adaptable animals. Many lynx starved while the foxes flourished. When the rabbit population recovered, the high fox population made it harder for the lynx to reestablish itself.

CONSERVATION MEASURES

● Following action measures ratified in Neuchâtel, Switzerland, in 1980, lynx have been released into the wild in Germany, Austria, Switzerland, Italy, and the former Yugoslavia. In Switzerland these are known to have been successful, with an estimated one hundred or so animals now roaming the wild; they have spread fairly extensively in the Swiss Alps and into France. Farmers have not greeted this success with enthusiasm,

Some 1,000 to 1,500 Spanish lynx survive today, forced to live in a shrinking habitat. Outside the Coto Doñana National Park, they are found only in a few upland areas. Even in Coto Doñana they are at risk, since the park's water sources are threatened by neighboring industries.

Eurasian lynx disappeared over much of their range during the 19th century, with major populations surviving only in the former U.S.S.R. and Scandinavia. Across the rest of its range, the lynx occurs only in isolated groups. Reintroduction projects have helped to revive it in some areas, but it has also begun to recolonize some areas naturally. Scandinavian and Russian lynx have, for example, gained a foothold in neighboring Finland.

SMALL CATS IN DANGER

THIS CHART SHOWS HOW THE INTERNATIONAL UNION FOR THE CONSERVATION OF NATURE (IUCN), OR THE WORLD CONSERVATION UNION, CLASSIFIED THE STATUS OF THE SMALL CATS OF EUROPE, ASIA, AND AFRICA:

SPANISH LYNX	ENDANGERED
BAY CAT	INSUFFICIENTLY KNOWN
CHINESE DESERT CAT	INSUFFICIENTLY KNOWN
PALLAS'S CAT	INSUFFICIENTLY KNOWN
MARBLED CAT	INSUFFICIENTLY KNOWN
FLAT-HEADED CAT	INSUFFICIENTLY KNOWN
RUSTY-SPOTTED CAT	INSUFFICIENTLY KNOWN
FISHING CAT	INSUFFICIENTLY KNOWN

ENDANGERED MEANS THAT THE ANIMAL IS IN DANGER OF EXTINCTION AND ITS SURVIVAL IS UNLIKELY UNLESS STEPS ARE TAKEN TO SAVE IT. INSUFFICIENTLY KNOWN MEANS THAT THE ANIMAL IS SUSPECTED, BUT NOT DEFINITELY KNOWN, TO BELONG TO ONE OF THE THREATENED CATEGORIES.

Eric Soder/NHPA

THE LYNX IS AT LAST BENEFITING FROM PROTECTION PROJECTS IN PARTS OF EUROPE.

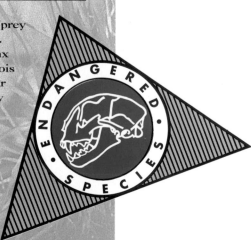

and even scrubland are fenced off, cultivated, and used for domestic agriculture; wetlands and swamps are drained and developed. Where an area of wilderness is not reclaimed for any of these reasons, it may nevertheless be rendered unsuitable for wildlife through pollution. This often applies to water habitats, affecting such wildcat species as the fishing cat and the flat-headed cat.

As habitats yield to civilization, their wild inmates are forced back into smaller areas. In the process, these areas become fragmented and isolated from one another; movement from one refuge to another is hindered by roads and other man-made barriers. Animals that do try to bridge such gaps are all too often the victims of traffic accidents; for those that remain, the chances of finding a suitable mate become increasingly remote, and local populations soon begin to suffer from inbreeding.

A CONFLICT OF INTERESTS

Even when areas are designated nature parks and preserves, conflicts may still arise. A national park and wildlife protection area was established, for example, on the island of Iriomote, which would support the Iriomote cat. However, much of the land along the lush valleys was reclaimed by settlers for growing rice and grazing livestock. The cats were forced back to the higher terrain, where they do not flourish as well because their principal prey animals tend to live lower down.

Few—if any—small cat species have escaped a decline in numbers through loss of habitat. The European wildcat, Asiatic golden cat, bay cat, leopard cat, fishing cat, flat-headed cat, Iriomote cat, marbled cat, and lynx have certainly all been hit

however, because they claim lynx prey on their sheep and other livestock. There are concerns also that lynx are preying on indigenous chamois and red deer populations. Similar concerns in other places, notably Germany, have confounded the reintroduction projects.

● Hunting bans, together with the establishment of preserves, have promoted an impressive recovery in lynx populations in Turkey.

Terry Whittaker/Frank Lane Picture Agency

hard. Populations of any wildcat species may also be seriously affected by fluctuations in their principal prey victims. A myxomatosis epidemic among rabbits in an area, for example, can have a dire effect on the wildcats that share the environment.

DOMESTIC STRIFE

The additional fact that some species can interbreed with domestic cats or feral cats can have an impact on the survival of the species. This is particularly true of the Eurasian wildcat, and the increase in its population in Scotland may be due in part to interbreeding with domestic cats rather than a true increase in the wild species. There are roughly seven million domestic cats in Britain; this is double the figure of twenty-five years ago, which means the chances of wildcats coming into contact with them have greatly increased.

Contact with domestic cats brings another hazard—that of disease. Wildcats are susceptible to most, if not all, the viruses and illnesses that affect domestic cats, as well as the range of parasites: lice, mites, ticks, and fleas. While in domestic animals these problems need only a quick visit to the vet, even comparatively minor ailments can easily kill wild animals. Luckily for cats, their solitary lifestyle helps to slow the spread of infectious diseases. ■

Zoologists can learn a great deal about cats, such as this Pallas's cat (right), from captive specimens.

The fishing cat (above) is still threatened by the fur trade, partly because of loopholes in local laws.

ALONGSIDE MAN

ANCIENT HEROES

Cats were domesticated by the Egyptians some 4,000 years ago, and they may have been members of human households even earlier than this. Cat remains were found in a settlement in Cyprus dating from about 7,000 years ago.

Although they lack the capacity for obedience that has made horses and dogs so useful to humans, cats nevertheless proved their worth from the start as controllers of rats, mice, and snakes. Whether it was this practical service or a religious association that prompted the Egyptians to domesticate cats is not known. Certainly they prized their cats highly: There was a city dedicated to the worship of Bastet, the Egyptian goddess who, in legend, took the earthly form of a cat. Cats were even mummified in tombs, along with other rodent-controlling species such as mongooses and birds of prey. Export in cats was forbidden— which, of course, initiated a lucrative smuggling trade, so that cats were soon widespread in the ancient world. Ever since, wherever humans have settled, cats have gone with them.

D. & R. Sullivan/Bruce Coleman Ltd.

INTO THE FUTURE

Too little is known about wildcats. Many live in areas of the world that simply lack the resources to study animals in the wild—the needs of humans take priority and animals must fend for themselves. In any event, studying small cats is particularly hard: They live mostly in remote areas and are usually active by night. The solitary nature of their lifestyles compounds the problem of gathering knowledge: Small cats will instinctively slink away from any contact with man, and while this is certainly a sound basis for self-preservation, it presents us with few learning opportunities.

Certainly, most of the small cats are protected legally in the wild, particularly if there is any doubt at all about their current status. They also benefit from the protection given to the high-profile animals, such as jaguars and tigers, with which they may share their habitat. Protected reserves set up

PREDICTION

A NEED TO KNOW MORE

Sheer lack of information hinders preservation of the small cats. Continuing encroachment upon remote wilderness areas will certainly wipe out small populations of certain species. Zoos are working with small cats to learn more about their basic biology and to establish some captive populations, but conservation must ultimately preserve viable habitats.

for such animals will offer similar protection to smaller species. But this is not really sufficient on its own. It is essential to have scientific data about an animal's lifestyle and habits in the wild in order to give it truly effective protection.

The Eurasian lynx is one of the few small cats that has benefited from modern technology, in the form of radiotelemetry. Many of those released into the wild have been fitted with collars with small but powerful radio transmitters, so their movements can be detected—normally from planes or off-road vehicles. The collars are designed to fit the cats as comfortably as possible. By radio-tracking lynx in the Swiss Alps, it was discovered, for example, that they wander over a vast area; males appeared to have ranges of 77–154 square miles (200–400 square kilometers). Few other small cats of Europe or Asia have been studied in this way; but there is a pressing need for it if sufficient information is to be discovered to ensure their survival. ∎

TEST-TUBE KITTENS

A species survival plan set up for particularly endangered species has achieved notable success with small cats. This is because some species are able to interbreed in some instances—many species of wildcats are known to be able to breed with domestic cats, for example. This means that domestic cats can function as surrogate mothers for embryos of rare wild species.

Successful experiments have already been undertaken with the European wildcat subspecies, the Indian desert cat. In one instance, eggs and sperm were taken from the wild animals and combined in the laboratory. The fertilized egg was inserted into the womb of a domestic cat, which later gave birth to Indian desert cat kittens.

BIG BROTHER'S HELP

An example of small cats benefiting from the protection given to their more familiar cousins is displayed at Sundarbans, a wetland habitat in Bangladesh. This great mangrove forest is noted for its population of more than 300 tigers, which prey on local deer and wild boar. The myriad waterways that drain through the swamps into the Bay of Bengal are an ideal habitat for the fishing cat, along with the rare Indian smooth-coated otter. As long as the locals of Sundarbans support the tiger, there is also a safe home for its smaller kin.

Illustration Kim Thompson

MANATEES

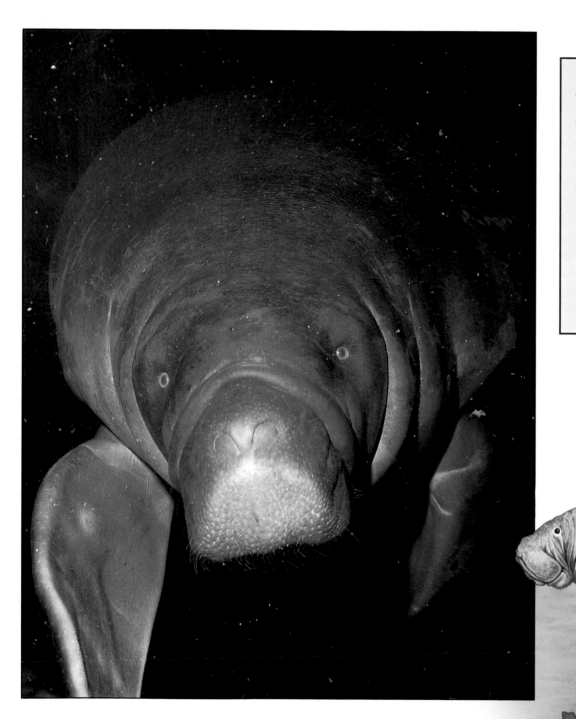

RELATIONS

The manatees and dugong comprise their own order, the Sirenia, which has no other members. Their closest living relatives include:

ASIAN ELEPHANT

AFRICAN ELEPHANT

Daniel J. Cox/Oxford Scientific Films

SIRENS OF THE SEA

IT IS HARD TO BELIEVE THAT MANATEES ONCE INSPIRED SAILORS TO DREAM OF MERMAIDS, BUT THESE HOARY GIANTS, WITH THEIR PLACID GAZE AND BLUBBERY BULK, ARE INDEED GENTLENESS PERSONIFIED

In 1493, during one of his voyages to the New World, the explorer Christopher Columbus was surprised, and not a little alarmed, to see a group of mermaids rising from the water off the coast of La Isla Española (today part of the Dominican Republic). He was forced to admit, however, that they were "not as beautiful as they are painted." The legend of the mermaids, or sirens, was well known to sailors at that time. These mythical creatures—half woman, half fish—were believed to lure seamen to their death at the bottom of the ocean, and this sighting must have caused a certain amount of panic on board the boat. Columbus and his crew had no need to worry, however, for these were not evil beings but merely a group of manatees—harmless aquatic mammals, with nothing more on their minds than eating sea grasses.

Columbus may have been the first, but he was certainly not the last person to mistake a manatee, or its close relative the dugong for a mermaid. Even as late as 1732, an Italian named Cavazzi wrote of a "fish-woman" he had encountered in a West African river, but his description describes nothing so accurately as a female dugong.

NEITHER FISH NOR WOMAN

Today there are three species of manatees—the West Indian, Amazonian, and West African manatees—and one species of dugong. Another species, Steller's sea cow, became extinct about 200 years ago. This was one of the largest known sirenians, reaching a length of up to 26 ft (8 m). It lived in cold, subarctic waters in the western Bering Sea and was hunted to extinction within twenty-seven years of its discovery in 1741. The four surviving species are all docile, plant-eating mammals that inhabit warm, tropical, and subtropical marine waters around the world.

Contrary to the belief of scientists right up until the 19th century, the manatees and dugong have no evolutionary relationship with any of the other major groups of living marine mammals, such as the whales, dolphins, porpoises, seals, walrus, and sea lions. In fact, they comprise their own order, Sirenia, a name that is obviously derived from their imaginary association with mermaids, or sirens.

Looking at the manatees today, it is difficult, if not impossible, to imagine how anyone could mistake them for alluring mermaids. They are huge, spindle-shaped creatures with short but highly mobile forelimbs. There are no hind limbs, although vestigial pelvic bones are evidence that they were once land-based animals. They do not even seem to have a neck, the blunt, rounded head apparently

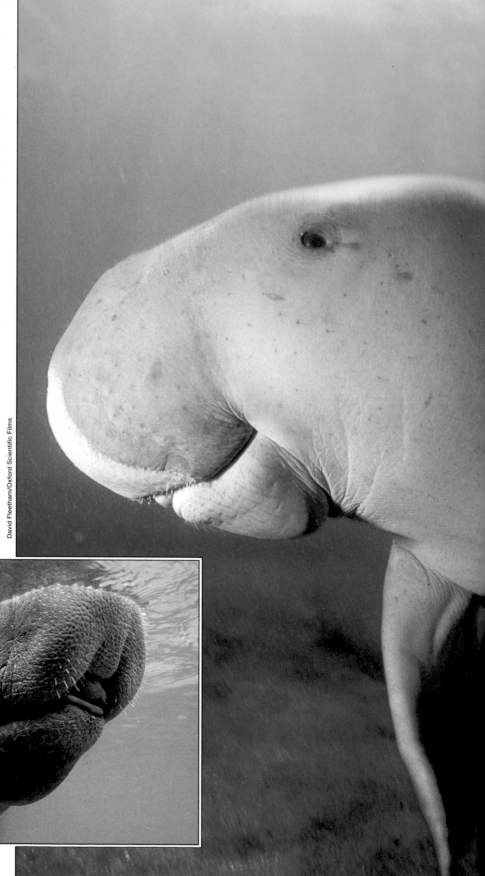

David Fleetham/Oxford Scientific Films

Douglas Faulkner/Oxford Scientific Films

Although their lungs are efficient, manatees still must surface every few minutes to breathe (above).

DISTANT RELATIVES

Sirenians are classified within the superorder Paenungulata, or subungulates, which also includes aardvarks, elephants, and hyraxes. Fossil evidence suggests that 60–25 million years ago all of these orders ascended from a common stock, one branch of which remained on land, while the other branch returned to the water.

Studies using biochemical analysis of proteins also suggest a common ancestry. Although externally these animals look very different from one another, all of the subungulates share certain anatomical features, including dental characteristics, lack of a clavicle (collarbone), and the presence of nails or hooves rather than primitive claws.

The sirenians' closest cousin is the elephant, the shape of the skull and the lower jaw being remarkably similar. The aquatic mammals' skin color, texture, and the arrangement of hairs is also similar to that of a young elephant, and the flattened flippers with their flat nails are vaguely reminiscent of an elephant's feet.

melting into the enormous blubbery body with just a few folds of fat in between. All three species have a rounded, paddle-shaped tail.

MODERN SIRENIANS

The West Indian manatee has three or four rudimentary "fingernails" on each flipper. Its rough skin is generally gray or brown, with sparse white hair scattered all over the body. Its eyes are small and located on the sides of the head. There is no external ear, just a tiny, almost invisible ear opening. Its snout has a distinctive downward slope, and there are stiff, bristling whiskers on the large, flexible upper lip. It measures 12–15 ft (3.7–4.6 m) in length and weighs about 3,500 lb (1,600 kg). The West African manatee is very similar to the West Indian manatee in terms of size, shape, and color. However, its eyes protrude more, and its snout is blunter and does not slope as much.

The Amazonian species is the smallest manatee, measuring 8–10 ft (2.5–3 m) and weighing some 770–1,100 lb (350–500 kg). Its skin is smoother than that of the other two, and it also has

The dugong's tiny eyes are protected underwater by oil-secreting glands in their lids.

distinctive white or pink patches on its belly and chest. Its flippers are longer, with no fingernails, and it has smaller teeth. It is the only sirenian that is confined solely to fresh water.

The dugong is also spindle shaped and gray, with hairs scattered all over its body. However, it differs from the manatees in that its skin is smooth and its tail is in the form of an indented fluke. The snout is distinctly turned down, and the deeply cleft upper lip protrudes beyond the lower lip, forming a U-shaped muscular pad that overhangs the mouth. This pad is called the rostral disk. The average length of a dugong is 9 ft (2.7 m) and weighs about 550–660 lb (250–300 kg).

All four sirenians are herbivorous (plant-eating) mammals. Despite their alarming size, they are gentle giants that always prefer to swim away from trouble rather than invite it. Sadly, they are all threatened species, and some of them are already extinct in parts of their range. ■

(A)NCESTORS

EARLY SIRENIANS

Sirenians probably originated as terrestrial animals in the Old World 50–45 million years ago. Within a few million years of their first appearance, the animals were completely aquatic and had begun to spread into new regions, including South America. The first animal to resemble the modern manatee was the *Potamosiren*, which dates from about 15 million years ago.

By about 5 million years ago, some populations were isolated in the Amazon Basin, and these gave rise to the modern Amazonian manatee. Others had migrated to the Caribbean and North America, giving rise to the two modern species, the West Indian and West African manatees. The second species probably evolved when some of the animals dispersed to Africa.

Fossils show that animals resembling dugongs were once widespread across western Europe, the Mediterranean, the Caribbean Sea, the southeastern United States, the Indian Ocean, South America, and the North Pacific.

THE SIRENIANS' FAMILY TREE

The order Sirenia is divided into two families: the manatees, Trichechidae, and the dugong, Dugongidae. There are two subspecies of West Indian manatees: the Florida and the Antillean manatees. Today there is only one species within the Dugongidae family; a second species, Steller's sea cow, became extinct about two hundred years ago.

WEST AFRICAN MANATEE
Trichechus senegalensis
(*trick-ECK-uss seh-ne-ga-LEN-sis*)

Very similar in appearance to the West Indian manatee, this species can be identified by its blunter, less downward-sloping snout and its more protuberant eyes.

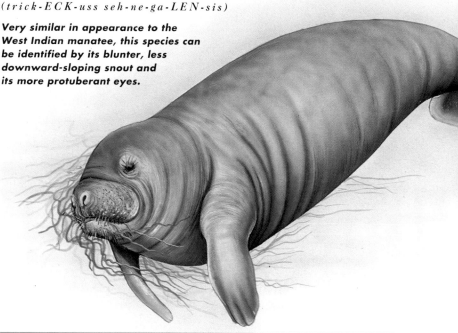

SIRENIANS

STELLER'S SEA COW

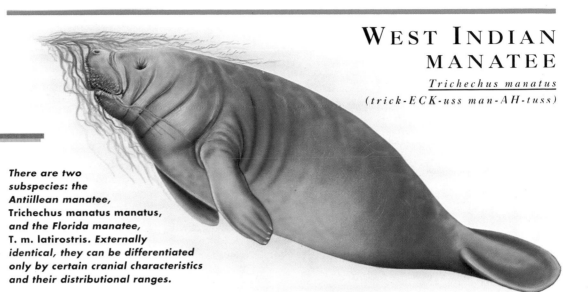

WEST INDIAN MANATEE
Trichechus manatus
(trick-ECK-uss man-AH-tuss)

There are two subspecies: the Antiillean manatee, Trichechus manatus manatus, and the Florida manatee, T. m. latirostris. Externally identical, they can be differentiated only by certain cranial characteristics and their distributional ranges.

MANATEES

SEA COWS

AMAZONIAN MANATEE
Trichechus inunguis
(trick-ECK-uss in-UN-gwis)

This is the smallest manatee, and the only species to be confined solely to freshwater habitats. It lacks the "fingernails" found on the flippers of the other two species. It is the most social species of manatee, gathering in groups of up to 100 where food is abundant.

DUGONG
Dugong dugon
(DOO-gong DOO-gon)

This is the most abundant sirenian species, distributed in the waters of forty-three countries along the western Pacific and Indian oceans. Its fluke-shaped tail is a key identifying feature.

Color illustrations Kim Thompson

ANATOMY:
THE MANATEE

DUGONG
There is a dip in the forehead, and the upper lip is less deeply cleft than in the manatees.

THE SNOUT
varies in profile according to species; this owes much to their differing feeding habits. In the manatees the upper lip is deeply cleft.

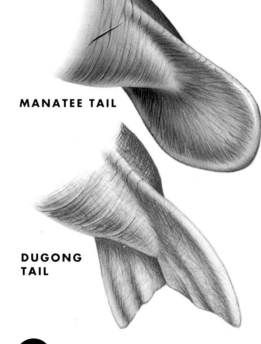

At about 26 ft (8 m) long, the extinct Steller's sea cow would have dwarfed all other sirenians. The largest species today is the West Indian manatee (top), which grows to 15 ft (4.6 m) and weighs up to 3,500 lb (1,600 kg). The dugong (above) is smaller, reaching about 13 ft (4 m) in length and a maximum weight of 2,000 lb (900 kg).

MANATEE TAIL

THE TEETH
move forward from the back of the jaw as they grow, dropping out when they reach the front. The manatee may lose up to thirty teeth during its lifetime, and this unique method of tooth replacement means that the animal always has sharp chewing surfaces.

DUGONG TAIL

All manatee species have a rounded, paddle-shaped tail. The tail of the dugong, however, is fluke shaped. All sirenians move their tails up and down to swim.

THE FRONT FLIPPERS
of the West Indian manatee are fairly short. They are also very flexible and have four "fingernails," which are lacking in the Amazonian manatee. The flippers are used to push food into the mouth, to touch other manatees, and to help the animal move over the sea- or riverbed.

X-RAY

six neck vertebrae

Manatee bones are extremely dense, and most lack marrow cavities. These dense bones act as ballast to offset the positive buoyancy caused by the large lungs and the intestinal gas generated during plant digestion. The sirenians' hand skeleton has five fingers.

MANATEE SKELETON

seven neck vertebrae

DUGONG SKELETON

barrel chest

five fingers

X-ray illustrations Elisabeth Smith

AMAZONIAN MANATEE

The snout of the Amazonian manatee does not slope down as markedly as those of other manatees.

WEST INDIAN MANATEE

As in other manatees, the upper lip is deeply cleft and bears stiff but sensitive bristles.

AFRICAN MANATEE

The broad snout angles down slightly. Both upper and lower lips bear stiff bristles.

THE SKIN

is generally gray or brown, but the color varies according to the type and amount of algae growing on it. It is rough and often covered by scars from injuries inflicted by propellers.

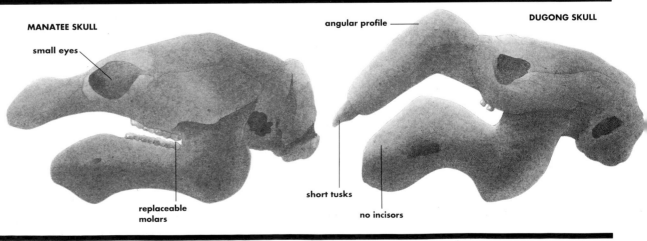

THE TAIL

is broad, paddle shaped, and huge in proportion to the body. Flipping it up and down, the manatee uses it like a paddle to move through the water.

Color illustrations Richard Tibbits

FACT FILE

WEST INDIAN MANATEE

CLASSIFICATION

GENUS: *TRICHECHUS*
SPECIES: *MANATUS*

SIZE

HEAD–BODY LENGTH: 12–15 FT (3.7–4.6 M)
WEIGHT: 3,500 LB (1,600 KG)
WEIGHT AT BIRTH: 44 LB (20 KG)
LENGTH AT BIRTH: 3.3 FT (1 M)

COLORATION

GRAY OR BROWN SKIN, WITH SPARSE WHITE HAIRS SCATTERED ALL OVER BODY AT INTERVALS OF 0.5 IN (1.27 CM)

FEATURES

NAILS ON FLIPPERS
DOWN-SLOPING SNOUT
BROAD, PADDLE-SHAPED TAIL
WHISKERS ON UPPER LIP

The skull of the dugong is about 24 in (61 cm) long. Its profile is more angular than that of the manatee, and it also has a pair of short tusks.

The manatee's skull is about 26 in (66 cm) long. It has only six neck vertebrae, whereas nearly all other mammals, including the dugong, have seven.

MANATEE SKULL

small eyes

replaceable molars

DUGONG SKULL

angular profile

short tusks

no incisors

WARM-WATER GRAZERS

MANATEES AND DUGONGS CANNOT ABIDE THE COLD, SO THEY ARE RARELY FOUND FAR FROM TROPICAL OR SUBTROPICAL WATERS. HERE, TOO, THEY FIND PLENTY TO EAT IN THE FORM OF LUSH VEGETATION

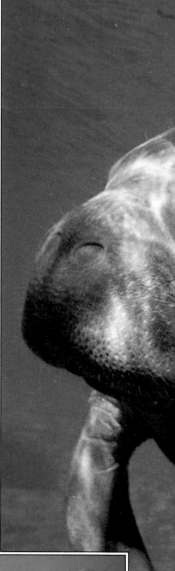

An inquisitive diver paddles quietly through the still waters of Crystal River in Florida. Without warning, a huge shadow parts from the waving strands of eelgrass and blots out the filtered light from the surface. Hanging from the corners of its mouth are the trailing ends of vegetation, its flexible snout undulating gently as it chews. Its monstrous body moves with surprising grace, and with barely a glance at the human intruder, the creature glides on by. This is a manatee, and this is how it spends up to eight hours every day—cropping copious amounts of underwater vegetation, pausing only briefly every few minutes to surface and breathe.

RESTING AND BREATHING

Manatees spend four or five hours of every day resting, either hanging vertically near the surface of the water or snuggled snout-first into the seabed in an almost trancelike state, rising to the surface every three or four minutes. They move up and down in the water column with apparently little effort, thanks to their ability to change the volume of their lungs by contracting or relaxing the diaphragm. A large resting manatee is able to stay underwater for up to twenty minutes, although smaller or more active individuals need to breathe more frequently. The Amazonian manatee, which is the smallest species, usually surfaces several times per minute to breathe, although one individual is reported to have stayed under for fourteen minutes.

Manatees breathe through two nostrils located on the tip of the snout, which means they do not even have to raise their head above the surface to take in air. In common with other aquatic mammals, these nostrils are valved and close up as soon as the animal submerges. Manatees renew about 90 percent of the air in their lungs in a single breath, unlike humans, who only renew about 10 percent,

and this means that breathing takes only a split second before the animal slips back below the surface.

Manatees are equally active by day or by night. When they are not resting or feeding, they often indulge in play, sometimes for up to twelve hours each day. They generally move slowly, about 1–4 mph (1.6–6.4 km/h), although when escaping from danger they are capable of short bursts of speed—sometimes more than 15 mph (25 km/h). They follow established travel routes and generally swim up to 10 ft (3 m) below the surface.

THE SHY DUGONG

Although herds of animals are often reported around the north Australian coastline, the dugong is generally a solitary animal. Extremely secretive and timid, it spends its days hidden in relatively deep off-

Nothing relieves a manatee's itchy back like a satisfying scratch on a stony riverbed (above).

Doug Perrine/Planet Earth Pictures

Douglas Faulkner/Oxford Scientific Films

MIGRATION

Manatees prefer a water temperature of about 68°F (20°C). Unusual for aquatic mammals, their blubber is an ineffective insulator, and sustained periods of severe cold weather will kill them. Paradoxically, in very cold weather they may stop eating, which depletes their blubber further, making them even more sensitive to cold. Another key factor in the manatees' failure to survive in very low temperatures is their extremely low metabolic rate, which they seem unable to increase sufficiently to compensate for heat loss.

To escape the cold, the Florida manatee migrates to natural and artificial warm-water refuges. There is a general shift south in winter, and some animals make special journeys to sites where they can be sure that the water will be cozy. For example, many of the manatees that spend the summer in northeastern Florida spend the winter in the warm water at the Riviera and Port Everglades power plants. Both the Amazonian and West African manatees move to deeper water when the water levels in their normal habitats drop during the dry season.

shore water. At night it moves into shallower water to feed until the first light of day. Although the maximum dive time for a dugong is eight minutes, most individuals are unable to stay underwater for long and have to breathe regularly every one or two minutes. Before breathing, a dugong will rise out of the water to look around for danger. If it sees an intruder, it quickly submerges again and swims away or hides in vegetation until the danger has passed. When it does breathe out, the dugong emits a surprisingly loud "phaa" sound, which can be heard from some distance away, giving a clue to the elusive animal's location.

Just like the manatees, the dugong swims by moving its tail up and down like a paddle, steering with its fins and by moving its head from side to side. It is a relatively slow swimmer, with a top speed of only about 5–6 mph (8–10 km/h). Despite its slow movements, the dugong is too large to have many predators, although sharks and killer whales have been known to attack it occasionally. ■

A manatee lifts a flipper to allow a calf access to her teats which, unusually, are set in the armpits.

HABITATS

All the living sirenians are aquatic animals, found only in warm tropical and subtropical waters. They rely on sea grasses or freshwater vegetation in order to survive, and their distribution therefore depends on where these plant materials are at their most abundant.

The two subspecies of West Indian manatees, although possessing different cranial characteristics, can be differentiated most easily by their range. As its name suggests, the Florida manatee can be found year-round off the coast of peninsular Florida in the United States. Its primary range along the Atlantic coast is from St. Johns River in the northeast to Miami in the south. On the Gulf coast it is abundant in Everglades National Park and extends northward to the Suwannee River. During the warm summer months, however, the Florida manatee may sometimes venture as far north as Virginia and as far west as Mississippi or Louisiana. Some animals have even been sighted in the waters of the Bahamas.

MANGROVES

The Florida Everglades are well stocked with distinctive mangrove swamps. Mangrove trees are evergreens with tough, leathery leaves and open-air root systems. These roots look and act rather like snorkels, enabling the trees to tolerate poorly

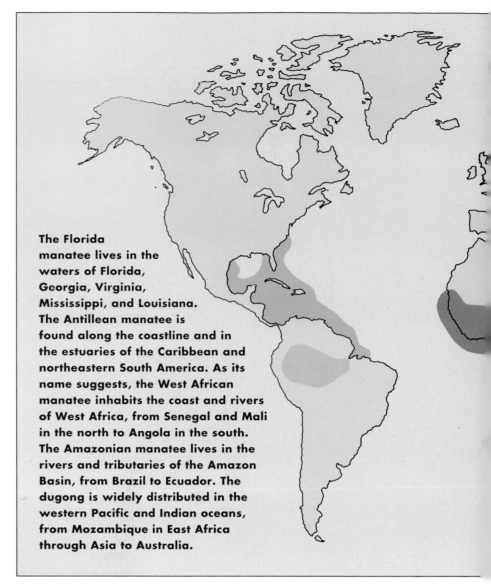

The Florida manatee lives in the waters of Florida, Georgia, Virginia, Mississippi, and Louisiana. The Antillean manatee is found along the coastline and in the estuaries of the Caribbean and northeastern South America. As its name suggests, the West African manatee inhabits the coast and rivers of West Africa, from Senegal and Mali in the north to Angola in the south. The Amazonian manatee lives in the rivers and tributaries of the Amazon Basin, from Brazil to Ecuador. The dugong is widely distributed in the western Pacific and Indian oceans, from Mozambique in East Africa through Asia to Australia.

Norbert Wu/NHPA

oxygenated soils, saltwater, and Florida's devastating hurricanes. There are three different types of mangroves. The red mangrove grows best in shallow salt water and spreads out into the sea. Its curving roots form a tough web that traps silt and, in time, creates a barrier against the sea behind which other plants can grow. The black mangrove grows in tidal zones. It has clusters of breathing pores that project into the air from the roots so that the tree can breathe during high tides and floods. The white mangrove is the most tolerant of freshwater and usually grows farther inland. It has few breathing pores and no supporting roots.

The Antillean manatee inhabits waters throughout the greater Caribbean area—including Mexico and southern Texas—and northeastern South America. Both subspecies can live in salt and fresh water, and any waterway that is over 3.3 ft (1 m) deep with a good supply of sea grasses or other vegetation can become home to a manatee. The West

The Lake Okeechobee–Everglades basin covers 17,000 sq mi (44,000 sq km), and the many rivers and connecting lakes are ideal for manatees (left).

DISTRIBUTION

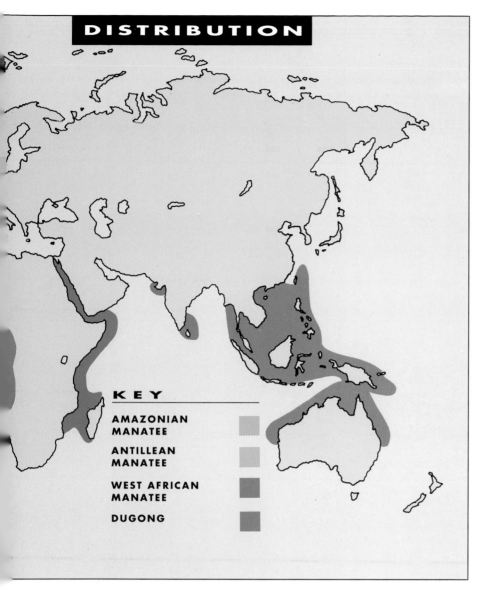

KEY

AMAZONIAN
MANATEE

ANTILLEAN
MANATEE

WEST AFRICAN
MANATEE

DUGONG

Nick Gordon/Ardea

(in)SIGHT

HEAT SEEKERS

Although the Florida manatee has always moved south to natural warm-water refuges for the winter, in recent years it has also been able to take advantage of man-made hot spots. The Florida coast is dotted with power plants that discharge warm water all year round. The manatees have become conditioned to expect warm water at these sites, and now many of them stay north of their historic wintering grounds, preferring instead to gather around these artificially heated sources. Sometimes, during especially cold weather, more than 200 manatees congregate at each water outlet. The power companies now find themselves laden with a huge responsibility toward the animals.

In December 1989, Florida experienced an unprecedented cold snap, with subzero temperatures lasting for several days. To escape the cold, many manatees headed for the warm outlets at the Florida Power and Light Company's power plants, instead of following their traditional migratory route south. Sadly, the air temperatures were so low that the water at the plants was not quite warm enough, and many manatees died. Now the company is looking into the possibility of creating a manatee "spa." This would be an enclosed area near the discharge, where the water could be kept at the correct temperature for the manatees without being cooled down by surrounding water currents.

Indian manatee can survive in bays, estuaries, rivers, and coastal areas, although it rarely ventures into deeper ocean waters.

During the winter, the Florida manatee migrates south to warmer water. The Blue Spring Run, a section of the St. Johns River in Blue Spring State Park near Orange City, Florida, is one of the most popular winter refuges. The attraction is the brilliantly clear water, which is kept at a constant 72°F (22°C) by warm water surging out of an underground spring at a rate of 100 million gallons (455 million liters) a day. Manatees have migrated here in the winter for thousands of years, and today the

Like other sirenians—and in fact like hippos, too—the Amazonian manatee possesses special valves that seal off its nostrils when diving.

park is an important winter refuge for over sixty individuals, many of which return every year and are well known to the rangers, who recognize them by scars on their backs. The manatees begin to arrive around mid-November, as soon as the water temperature in the main part of the river reaches 68°F (20°C), and they stay until sometime in March.

The West African manatee can also live in fresh or saltwater. It generally prefers quiet coasts, broad rivers, lagoons, and connected lakes. In Senegal, the manatee sometimes moves so far upstream in the Senegal River that it gets trapped in tributaries and lakes by dwindling water levels in the dry season. In these cases, staff from the Ministry of Water and Forests take the isolated manatees back to the river.

The Amazonian manatee is the only sirenian confined to freshwater. It lives in the myriad rivers of the Amazon Basin and is most abundant in floodplain lakes and channels in white-water (less acidic) river systems. Its preferred water temperature is around 77–86°F (25–30°C). During the wet season the manatee is widely dispersed throughout its range; but as the water levels drop during the dry season, animals begin to congregate in deep-water

lakes and deep parts of rivers, where they remain until the rains return and the water levels rise.

The dugong is chiefly a salt-water animal, but it is sometimes found in estuaries. It occurs in the waters of forty-three countries along the western Pacific and Indian Oceans and is most abundant in the northern half of Australia, where an estimated 70,000 individuals may live. Like the manatees, the dugong prefers shallow water, and although dives of up to 36–40 ft (11–12 m) have been observed, these are rare. ∎

Doug Perrine/Planet Earth Pictures

FOCUS ON

FLORIDA'S EVERGLADES

The Florida Everglades is an immense national park covering some 13,000 sq mi (33,670 sq km). It comprises various habitats including marshy grasslands, pine forests, and the mangrove swamps that are home to the Florida manatee. In addition to the manatee, the Everglades mangroves support the raccoon, coon oyster, roundtailed muskrat, sea turtle, tree snail, and many snakes.

The Everglades has a summer wet season from May to October and a winter dry season. During the former there is heavy rainfall and the atmosphere is warm and humid. This is also the hurricane season. During the dry season, water levels in the park fall dramatically, and the manatee migrates to deeper waters.

TEMPERATURE AND RAINFALL

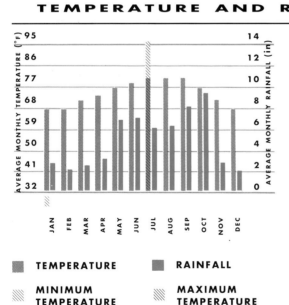

TEMPERATURE

RAINFALL

MINIMUM TEMPERATURE

MAXIMUM TEMPERATURE

The data here apply to the Miami area, on the southernmost tip of Florida. Temperatures and rainfall peak in the summer months, but most months see an appreciable amount of rainfall. Florida is sunnier, and has more thunderstorms, than any other state in the United States. Although conditions are generally stable throughout the year, occasional cold snaps in January can cause problems for the manatees.

NEIGHBORS

Florida's subtropical habitats are a rich, fertile environment for plants and animals. They are home to at least 100 different mammal species, including armadillos, bears, and big cats.

ROYAL TERN

The royal tern feeds on fish and crabs. It breeds along the coasts of the Americas and West Africa.

AMERICAN ALLIGATOR

A ferocious predator, the American alligator lives in the warm swamps of the southeastern United States.

Neighbor illustrations Robin Charter/Wildlife Art Agency. Alligator Tracey A. Stitch/Wildlife Art Agency

FLORIDA

Much of Florida lies on a peninsula that projects some 500 mi (800 km) into the Atlantic Ocean and forms the eastern lip of the Gulf of Mexico. The land is low lying, the highest point rising only 345 ft (105 m) above sea level. South of the Everglades and Florida Bay lie the Keys, a long chain of tiny islands.

GEORGIA

Atlantic Ocean

Gulf of Mexico

FLORIDA

Everglades

SWAMPY AREAS

LEMON SHARK

The stealthy lemon shark cruises the shallow coastal waters on the lookout for good-sized fish to eat.

SNAPPING TERRAPIN

The snapping terrapin possesses immensely powerful jaws that can kill even a baby alligator.

SPOTTED GROUPER

A master of disguise, the spotted grouper can change color in seconds to avoid its enemies.

MARSH HAWK

As hunters of frogs, small birds, and insects, hawks find a rich supply of prey in the Everglades swamps.

BELTED KINGFISHER

This winter resident of the Everglades is a solitary and deadly predator of freshwater fish.

FOOD AND FEEDING

The sirenians are often referred to as sea cows, a name derived partly from their cattlelike docility but also from their diet. Just like cattle, manatees and dugongs are herbivores, feeding on a wide variety of aquatic vegetation found in their saltwater or freshwater environment.

In salt water, the West Indian manatee generally feeds on sea grasses, as well as mangrove leaves and various algae. In freshwater, it eats water hyacinth, wild celery, and water milfoil.

The West Indian manatee is a flexible feeder, consuming food from the bottom, the middle, and the surface of the water. It has even been known to haul itself partially out of the water to get at tasty bank vegetation and tempting leaves on overhanging branches. The Amazonian and West African manatees, on the other hand, feed only on floating grasses, as their native waters are often too dark for plants to grow beneath the surface. These different feeding habits have resulted in the development of different-shaped snouts. The West Indian manatee has a downward-sloping snout, which enables it to feed on plants growing close to the ground.

in SIGHT

JOBS FOR MANATEES

The manatees' voracious appetite has led to the suggestion that they be used to clear weeds and help keep waterways open. Between 1954 and 1974, over 200 manatees were placed in weed-choked waterways in Guyana, where they were remarkably effective in keeping the weeds under control. Unfortunately, the manatees began to go hungry, and many of them were poached, so eventually the project was abandoned.

Inspired by the relative success of the project in Guyana, many other countries have expressed an interest in using manatees to clear weed-clogged channels, and experiments have taken place in the United States and Mexico. Unfortunately the experiments met with little success. One of the main problems is the manatees' need for warmth. Once the water becomes too cold for them, they are obliged to leave the area—and its rapidly growing weeds—for several months at a time.

Manatees spend up to eight hours a day grazing. They have voracious appetites and eat up to 11 percent of their body weight each day. Swimming slowly through the water, a manatee will use its flippers to grasp food and push it into its mouth, where it is broken up by the thick, ridged pads at the front of the mouth before being pushed to the sides where it is chewed by the grinding molars. The large upper lip is deeply split, with both halves acting independently, like forceps, to grip food tightly.

Many of the manatee's food plants are tough and fibrous. To cope with this, it has developed a method of constantly replacing worn teeth. The molars move forward from the back to the front of

John Morris/Wildlife Art Agency

SEA PIGS

Dugongs (below) *are sometimes called "sea pigs" because they use their large snouts to dig up their favorite food—the roots of sea grasses—from the seabed.*

West Indian manatees (left) are flexible feeders and have the most varied diet among sirenians.

Doug Perrin/ Planet Earth Pictures

the mouth at a rate of about 0.04 in (1 mm) per month. When they reach the front of the mouth, they drop out. Elephants have the same feature.

Despite their hearty appetites, manatees are able to go without food for a considerable length of time. During the winter when the weather is colder and food is scarcer, the Florida manatee will become relatively inactive in an effort to conserve energy, and it may even fast completely for a week or more. During the dry season, when aquatic plants are unavailable, the Amazonian manatee may fast for up to six months, surviving on fat stored as blubber.

The dugong is also a herbivore, feeding strictly on aquatic vegetation, usually at night. Although it eats the whole plant, it favors the carbohydrate-rich roots, which it digs from the bottom with its snout. An adult dugong may eat up to one-tenth of its body weight each day, and at low tide it is often possible to follow the path of a dugong by examining its feeding trails through the sea-grass beds.

Before eating a plant, the dugong will shake it to remove sand or coral, similar the way that its distant relative, the elephant, cleans its food. The dugong may also pile the plants into heaps and leave them for a few minutes to allow the sand to drop out and any hidden sea animals to escape. ■

ALMOST TOOTHLESS

Tough pads on the upper and lower palates allow the dugong to chew its food. Unlike manatees, whose teeth are constantly renewed, dugongs have only a few peglike molars at the back of the jaw.

TERRITORY

Except for when large numbers of animals congregate at warm-water refuges during the winter, the only lasting association manatees are likely to form is that between a female and her calf. When manatees do swim together, however, they generally move in single file; although a calf will always swim parallel to its mother, just behind her flipper. It is believed that this position enables the animals to communicate most effectively and also cuts down on the drag from the water on the calf.

The Amazonian manatee is probably the most social species, often living in groups of four to eight. Occasionally it will be found in large groups, sometimes numbering several hundred animals. These groups probably form in response to local ecological conditions such as food, temperature, and water levels, rather than from any specific social need.

Manatees are not aggressive animals. If they are threatened, their first instinct is to swim away from the danger. Even when a calf is approached by humans, the most its mother will do is swim between the intruder and her offspring.

COMMUNICATION

Sound plays a key part in manatee communication. When the animals are frightened, sexually aroused, playing, or swimming with calves, they emit squeaks, squeals, chirps, and whistles that are produced in the larynx and are audible to humans. Vocalization plays a large part in keeping a mother and calf together, and many observers have reported a "duet" between the pair, where the two animals

A manatee mother and calf playing (right). *There is a strong bond between the two.*

Douglas Faulkner/Oxford Scientific Films

SCENT MARKING

Manatees rub themselves against underwater rocks as a way of leaving a scent messages. It is thought that females scent mark to advertise their readiness to mate.

KISS HELLO

For manatees, kissing is a form of greeting. It also helps the animals recognize one another.

chirp to one another in turn. This song is especially important when escaping from danger. It has also been suggested that certain calls are used to warn of danger and to keep herds together during flight.

It is also believed that manatees use infrasound (frequencies too low to be heard by humans) as a form of communication, and it is likely that a receptive female emits infrasound to attract males. Some scientists believe that manatees also employ echolocation (the process of emitting sound pulses and reading the returning echoes) to find their way through the often murky waters of their environment. This has yet to be proved, however.

Touch is important to manatees. There is a great deal of body contact between

KEY FACTS

● When several manatees get together, especially when they are well fed and free from danger, they indulge in what some scientists believe to be play. They will bolt and turn, grasp one another with their fins, and may even "kiss" snout to snout.

● Sometimes a group of manatees will body surf, riding the strong currents that occur below flood dams when the gates are partly open. They may drift with the current, turn their bodies sideways to it, or cut diagonally back and forth across it, but they always maintain their position parallel to one another. This behavior sometimes lasts more than an hour, and the manatees often nuzzle one another and vocalize throughout.

individuals, especially a mother and her calf, and they also seek contact with inanimate objects such as rocks. Some will even approach divers and spend a long time brushing up against them. The 1- to 2-in (2.5- to 5-cm) hairs that are scattered over their bodies enable the manatees to detect the touch of other animals or water movements created by other animals nearby.

Manatees have often been seen rubbing themselves against underwater rocks and logs. In fact, observations of known individuals who return to the same warm-water refuges every winter have revealed that they often use the same "rubbing posts" year after year. If this object disappears, the animal will choose a new one in or near the same location. The parts of the body that they rub are the genitalia, the area around the eyes, the armpits, and the chin—all areas where glandular secretions occur—which suggests that what these animals are doing is scent-marking.

SAFETY IN NUMBERS

Very little is known about the social behavior of the dugong. It often forms large herds of several hundred animals, and it is likely that the female and her calf are the core of the social group, as in the manatee. These herds may be formed as a means of protection against sharks and other predators and are probably also important in teaching young animals about feeding grounds and safe swimways. ∎

Color illustration Andy Peck/Wildlife Art Agency

LIFE CYCLE

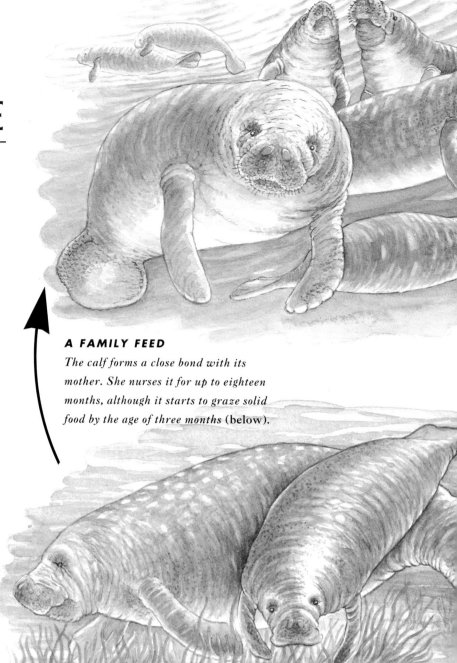

Manatees are at best semisocial animals, with most groupings occurring only at warm-water refuges during the winter. When a female is sexually receptive, however, she becomes the focus of attention for a group of a dozen or more males, who follow her around for up to a month, jostling agitatedly for position and the chance to be the first to mate with her. The female seems an unwilling participant; she does her utmost to avoid her suitors by twisting, turning, and tail-slapping. She may even swim into dangerously shallow water in her efforts to escape. Eventually, however, she succumbs—and usually to more than one male. After mating, the males disperse to look for other receptive females. They play no further part in the life of the mother or her calf.

BIRTH OF A MANATEE

Although breeding occurs all year round, it is often timed so that the calf is born when food supplies are at their peak. Gestation lasts 12–13 months and generally produces one calf, which is almost always born tail first, although breech births do occasionally occur; a few cases of twins have been reported. The calf of the West Indian and West African manatee is about 47 in (119 cm) long and weighs 65 lb (30 kg). Amazonian manatee calves are somewhat smaller. Although the fetuses are covered in hair, the newborn animal is completely hairless. Observers often report that the mother assists her newborn calf to the surface to take its first breath. However, scientists now believe that the calf is able to swim to the

A FAMILY FEED
The calf forms a close bond with its mother. She nurses it for up to eighteen months, although it starts to graze solid food by the age of three months (below).

surface by itself and that the female is just exhibiting attentive maternal behavior.

The female's mammary glands are located in an axillary (armpit) position, not too far from the pectoral (chest) position in humans. This has given rise to some imaginary tales of the mother cradling her calf in her "arms" while it suckles, but this is wholly untrue: The calf lies beside its mother, just below her flipper. It begins to nurse a few hours after birth and usually suckles for up to three minutes at a time, taking in milk, which is rich in proteins, fats, and salt. Although the calf will begin to eat vegetation within a few weeks of the birth, it will not be completely weaned for 12–18 months, during which time it will learn from its mother about migration routes, food, and feeding areas.

Sirenians have a low reproductive rate, and a twin birth is an extremely rare occurrence (left).

Douglas Faulkner/Oxford Scientific Films

GROWING UP
The life of a West Indian manatee

RELUCTANT PARTNER

A sexually receptive female is chased by up to seventeen males at once, who all try to be first to mate with her (left). She tries to get away, but eventually gives in to at least one of her ardent suitors.

SECRET BIRTH

The expectant female seeks out a sheltered backwater in which to give birth. The instant the calf is born (right), she nuzzles it to the surface to take its first gulp of air.

TAKING MILK

The mother's teats are located in the armpits, so her calf swims slowly alongside to suckle from her (right).

Manatees breed slowly, which is one of the reasons they are so rare. They do not reach sexual maturity before the age of six years, and a female will usually give birth only once every two years.

DUGONGS

The mating behavior of the dugong is similar to that of the manatees, but it differs in one significant respect. As with the manatees, a receptive dugong female is hotly pursued by a group of mature males, but in this case the males are far more aggressive. They claim territories, which they staunchly defend, engaging in violent combat with rivals in attempts to win breeding rights. This is the only time when the otherwise docile dugong shows any kind of aggression, but many males bear the scars that confirm that this is no mere display of bravado.

The dugong calf stays with its mother for up to two years, often riding on her back to feed. Adults reach sexual maturity fairly late in life, sometimes not until the age of 18 years, and this, coupled with the fact that a female is unlikely to produce more than five or six calves during her long life, is a key reason why the dugong is threatened. ■

FROM BIRTH TO DEATH

WEST INDIAN MANATEE	AMAZONIAN MANATEE
GESTATION: 13 MONTHS	**GESTATION:** 13 MONTHS
NO OF YOUNG: 1	**NO OF YOUNG:** 1
LENGTH AT BIRTH: 47 IN (119 CM)	**LENGTH AT BIRTH:** 33–41 IN (85–105 CM)
WEIGHT AT BIRTH: 65 LB (30 KG)	
SEXUAL MATURITY: BOTH SEXES 6–8 YEARS	**SEXUAL MATURITY:** BOTH SEXES 6–8 YEARS
LONGEVITY: 50 YEARS	**LONGEVITY:** 50 YEARS

DUGONG	WEST AFRICAN MANATEE
GESTATION: 13 MONTHS	**GESTATION:** 13 MONTHS
NO OF YOUNG: 1	**NO OF YOUNG:** 1
LENGTH AT BIRTH: 39–47 IN (100–120 CM)	**LENGTH AT BIRTH:** 47 IN (119 CM)
SEXUAL MATURITY: MALE 9–10 YEARS, FEMALE 9–18 YEARS	**WEIGHT AT BIRTH:** 65 LB (30 KG)
	SEXUAL MATURITY: BOTH SEXES 6–8 YEARS
LONGEVITY: 50 YEARS	**LONGEVITY:** 50 YEARS

Illustrations Carol Roberts

SUNSET SIREN SONG

HUNTED FOR GENERATIONS FOR THEIR MEAT, THE MANATEES AND DUGONG ARE ALSO RAPIDLY LOSING GROUND AS HUMANS USURP THEIR DWINDLING HABITATS. IS IT TOO LATE NOW TO SAVE THEM?

ll four sirenian species are currently facing the threat of extinction. While the reasons for this threat are complex and diverse, they are all to some extent engendered by mankind.

Although the West Indian manatee has never been hunted commercially, it has long been culled by local people for its meat. In fact, archaeological evidence shows that the manatee was hunted as long ago as the Paleo-Indian period (8500–6000 B.C.). Subsistence hunting continued until the end of the 19th century, at which time the manatee was also being hunted on a relatively small scale to provide specimens for museums and aquariums.

Today, although hunting is illegal throughout the West Indian manatee's range, the species is in danger of extinction, although this time the problem is the rapidly rising human population. Every day, 1,000 new residents move into Florida, and most of

> SPEEDBOATS HAVE NO PLACE IN THE ECOSYSTEM OF THE PONDEROUS, PLACID MANATEE, AND CONFLICT IS INEVITABLE

these people end up living on, or close to, the coast. To keep up with this population boom, much of Florida's wilderness is being turned into houses, stores, and power plants, and the manatee's available habitat is shrinking accordingly.

Water sports, too, are having a disastrous effect. There are about 700,000 boats currently registered in Florida, with another 400,000 from other regions using Florida's waters. Almost every manatee in Florida is covered with scars caused by propellers, and aquariums in the state are full of animals recuperating from horrific boat-inflicted injuries. Collisions with motorboats is by far the greatest single human-related cause of Florida manatee mortality today.

The Antillean manatee is also being threatened by human activity. Much of its habitat has been lost to settlements, and the population has been considerably reduced by poachers.

AMAZONIAN SLAUGHTER

For centuries, the Amazonian manatee has been the prey of subsistence hunters who need to feed their families. Manatee meat is still an important source of food for many local tribes, and although hunting the animal has been illegal since 1973, the practice continues to this day.

Kurt Amsler/Planet Earth Pictures

Today, manatees are a subject of scrutiny by both curious tourists and concerned biologists (above).

Nick Gordon/Survival Anglia

THEN & NOW

This map shows the current and former ranges of the West Indian manatee.

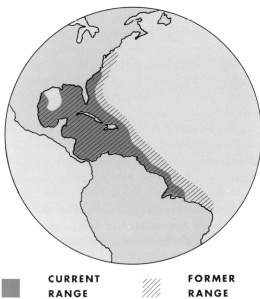

■ **CURRENT RANGE**   ▨ **FORMER RANGE**

The West Indian or American manatee was once common and widespread throughout the coastal and riverine waters of the southeastern United States, Central America, and northern South America.

Despite being protected, the species has drastically declined in numbers during this century, and its range has contracted accordingly. The chief threats have come from hunting, pollution, entanglement in fishing tackle, and collision with the propellers of powerboats.

While subsistence hunting probably has a modest impact on the status of the Amazonian manatee, it was the wholesale slaughter for commercial gain that had the most damaging effect on the species. Between 1600 and 1973, hundreds of thousands of Amazonian manatees were killed for the profit on their flesh, with disastrous effects on the population. Although there was concern for the species' survival as early as the 18th century, the killing continued at an annual rate of 1,000–2,000 into this century. Indeed, during the hunting peak of the 1950s, the meat industry accounted for almost 7,000 manatee deaths each year.

Although some illegal subsistence hunting is still practiced today, the main threat to the Amazonian manatee is that of habitat destruction. Deforestation

Like all of its wild neighbors, the Amazonian manatee is put at risk by local deforestation.

more complicated. Each of these species is found in more than one country, which makes it difficult to coordinate conservation efforts. Indeed, in some cases the species' host countries are at war with one another, which utterly confounds any cooperation in the field of conservation. Another problem is that most of these countries are economically disadvantaged compared to the United States, which means that saving the manatees is far from the top of their list of priorities. In addition, in several areas, such as Amazonia, the manatees' habitat is rapidly being destroyed, while in other countries, such as Gambia, it is being altered by the damming of rivers, with disastrous consequences.

In every country in which the sirenians are found, there is some degree of national or local legislation designed to protect them. The West African manatee, for example, is protected under Class A of the African Convention for the Conservation of Nature and Natural Resources, which was originally signed by thirty-eight African countries. In Guyana, manatees have been protected since 1956. Implementing the legislation, however, is an uphill struggle. In Cameroon, West Africa, manatee hunting is illegal, but this does not stop neighboring Nigerians from crossing the border, killing the manatees, and then selling the meat back to the Cameroonians.

SETTING AN EXAMPLE

But there are rays of hope for the manatees. In Ecuador, for example, the Siona Indians have hunted the Amazonian manatee for food for thousands of

ALONGSIDE MAN

Sirenians have always been hunted for their meat, which apparently tastes like beef or veal, but over the centuries people have found a use for almost every other part of the body. The thick hide, for example, can be made into shields, whips, and other durable leather goods. Between 1935 and 1954, up to 100,000 Amazonian manatees were killed for their hides, which were tanned and made into machinery belts, gaskets, and hoses for industry. The manatees' bones are thick and heavy, which made them ideal as weapons or for carving, while the fat has long been used for cooking or medicine. In the 16th century, Spanish settlers in the New World believed that the bones of the manatee's inner ear had wonderful medicinal properties and were able to cure stomach pains. To this day in Panama, the ground bones are used to alleviate the pain of childbirth.

Besides the belief that sirenians are mermaids, there are many other legends associated with them. The Rama Indians of Nicaragua used to bathe in manatee blood after a hunt; while in Cameroon, West Africa, some fishermen believe that manatees are evil and receive power from the Devil.

years, using traditional skills passed down from father to son. But today the manatee population has become so reduced that the Siona tribe has voluntarily ceased its hunting practices in an effort to protect the few remaining individuals. Wildlife authorities hope that examples such as this will become more common, and they are increasing their efforts to educate people about manatee conservation throughout the animals' range.

SAVING THE DUGONG

Just like the manatees, the dugong is also protected by national laws in all of the countries whose waters it inhabits. Unfortunately, it often proves difficult to enforce these laws, and the dugong population is seriously reduced in much of its range, especially in those poorer countries where dugong conservation is of little—if any—importance to the local people.

In Australia and Papua New Guinea, where dugong hunting is important in native tradition and culture, local tribespeople are working with wildlife authorities in an effort to preserve their traditions and maintain a viable dugong population. Wildlife officials are trying to introduce hunting quotas and are encouraging hunters to avoid pregnant females or females with dependent calves.

There is also a need to protect dugong habitat from human activities, and the Great Barrier Reef Marine Park Authority has been instrumental in setting up various reserves. Sadly, in countries such as India and Sri Lanka, civil war and poverty have prevented similar successes in these areas. ■

The "tears" of this captive dugong in Irian Jaya are "milked" in the belief that they serve as an aphrodisiac.

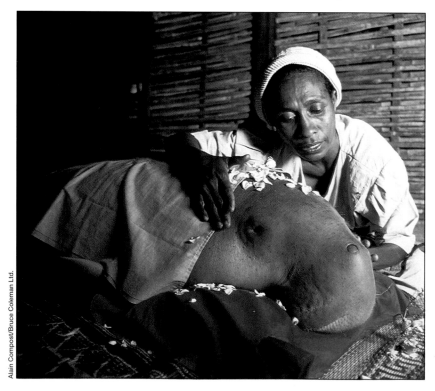

Alain Compost/Bruce Coleman Ltd.

INTO THE FUTURE

In many of the countries where sirenians live, scientists are desperate to gather information before it is too late. The best-studied species is the West Indian manatee, and there are many research projects currently under way, most of them based in Florida. The primary center of dugong research is in Townsville, Australia, while the Amazonian manatee is being studied by the Projecto Peixe-Boi in Brazil. Until scientists have enough data on the sirenians' population numbers, range, and behavior, it will be difficult to set up conservation programs.

An increasing threat to the West African manatee is river damming. A growing number of dams are being constructed for hydroelectric power, flood control, and irrigation, and, as the manatees move up and down rivers, they are prevented from moving along their normal routes; some are even crushed by the devices used by the dams.

Illustration Evi Antoniou

PREDICTION

SLOW BREEDING IS A SETBACK
Even if all the threats are eventually reduced, sirenians breed so slowly that they will probably never restore their numbers to historical levels. At present, the Florida manatee is the only species with a real chance of long-term survival.

A major impediment to sirenian conservation is that the animals are found in the waters of so many different countries, many of which are at war with one another. These logistical handicaps are coupled with the fact that many of the sirenians' host countries are too poor to support their native wildlife when human needs are so pressing. Ironically, these countries will be all the poorer if their wildlife and other natural resources are not protected.

With the exception of the Florida manatee, whose future looks comparatively rosy, the prospect for the sirenians is bleak. Their secretive nature and highly international range makes it impossible to conduct accurate censuses, but most experts agree that their populations are still on the decrease. In many parts of their historical range, manatees and dugongs have already been wiped out, and there is a widespread belief that, despite the conservation measures currently being implemented around the world, it may be too late to save the sirenians from total extinction. ∎

CAPTIVE HUSBANDRY

Because all sirenians are endangered, few are held in captivity unless they are part of research or rehabilitation programs. Three facilities in Florida—the Miami Seaquarium, Sea World, and Lowry Park Zoo—are authorized by the U.S. Fish and Wildlife Service to manage manatees with an aim to return them eventually to the wild. Manatees are tagged before release, and they are often also fitted with radio transmitters that enable biologists to follow their progress. So far, all of the releases have been successful.

Captive-born manatees are of great interest to scientists, who can find out more about breeding habits and the behavior of female-and-calf pairs. Manatees breed well in captivity—to date, eight have been born at the Seaquarium—but they do so slowly, and there is still much to be learned about their lifestyle.

SAVE THE MANATEE

Based in Florida, the Save the Manatee Club was set up in 1981 to increase public awareness. It started by sending speakers and educational material to community groups and schools. Then in 1984 it launched its Adopt-a-Manatee program, in which, for $15, members received a description and photograph of a manatee they had "adopted." Today the club has about 30,000 members worldwide and has become a powerful voice for the conservation of the manatee. Many of the club's recommendations have been incorporated into rules designed to protect the species. In addition, the club distributes thousands of press kits to newspapers, magazines, and TV and radio stations across America.

MARTENS

Wayne Lankinen/Aquila

DEADLY FINESSE

MARTENS AND MINKS MAY LOOK GRACEFUL, BUT TO THEIR SMALLER NEIGHBORS IN THE FORESTS AND WETLANDS THEY ARE LETHAL ENEMIES, CAPABLE OF INFLICTING DEATH AT A HALF-SECOND'S NOTICE

Methodically efficient, the marten is equaled by few other predators in its speed of attack. Always alert, with razor-sharp senses, it combines the agility of a squirrel with the predatory finesse of a cat. Its short legs and long body—typical of the weasel family to which it belongs—allow it to slip into tree holes and crevices to flush out likely prey, and its flexible spine, another weasel trait, enables it to bend almost double to slip out of tight corners.

Yet although the pine marten has much in common with its weasel relatives there is scant chance of mistaking it, for it is far bigger—almost the size of a small domestic cat. Unlike the weasels and stoats it has not become a specialist at diving into tunnel systems after burrowing rodents, so it has not developed their low-profile, cylindrical body form.

Indeed fossil evidence suggests that its shape has hardly changed for thirty million years, and its skeletal anatomy resembles that of the first carnivores of

The minks and martens are carnivores. They are part of the Mustelidae family, which also includes weasels, polecats, skunks, otters, badgers, and the wolverine. The martens and minks are classified in the subfamily Mustelinae, and consist of eight species of martens and two species of mink. The subfamily also includes the twenty-one species of weasel and polecat, and the wolverine.

ORDER

Carnivora (carnivorous mammals)

FAMILY

Mustelidae (weasels and their allies)

SUBFAMILY

Mustelinae (weasels and polecats)

GENERA

two

SPECIES

eight marten species

two mink species

in SIGHT

SHORT LEGACY

Compared to their length, martens and minks seem to have absurdly short legs. There is good reason for this. Like all the mustelids (members of the weasel family), they have inherited a body plan that is good for hunting in tree holes and burrows. But since martens and minks are not dedicated burrow hunters like the weasels and polecats, and often find themselves pursuing prey in the open, why have they retained short limbs? One reason is their arboreal lifestyle. Another is that short limbs are an adaptation for pursuing small prey.

Still another reason is that they have highly flexible spines. Originally developed for maneuverability in a tight squeeze, the spine allows the whole body to be bent and extended as the animal bounds along, and this provides the long stride that a dog, say, obtains by extending its long legs.

all—the compact, nimble, tree-dwelling Vulpavines that hunted through the trees in the forests of America some fifty or sixty million years ago. The pine marten and its allies have continued this ancestral trade—although they also hunt on the ground—and as a result they have altered little since that era when the dust had barely settled on the footprints of the last dinosaurs. But this does not mean that they are primitive. It just shows how efficient and versatile they are, and always were.

There have been some changes in the marten dynasty, though. The fossilized remains of martens dating from about five million years ago begin to fall into three groups matching those found today: the pine marten and its allies in the northern forests, the American fisher, and the tropical yellow-throated martens. From about two million years ago the features of the eight modern species begin to appear, although the distinctions are so subtle that some zoologists are inclined to treat all modern martens as racial variations on the original trio theme.

EVER-DECREASING MARTENS

This point of view is supported by the martens themselves, which may interbreed if they get the opportunity. At the eastern limit of its range, in the great dark conifer forests of central Siberia, the pine

Largest of all the martens, the fisher or Virginian polecat is widespread across North America.

Alan & Sandy Carey/Oxford Scientific Films

Bibs help to identify species; the yellow-throated marten (below), *for example, has bold markings.*

E. & D. Hosking/Frank Lane Picture Agency

marten may mate with the similar but smaller sable to produce a hybrid called the kida. Farther east the sable's range overlaps with that of the even-smaller Japanese marten, and the diminishing size trend continues with the American marten, the smallest of all. The difference between an American marten and a pine marten is quite marked, but moving east around the northern hemisphere the differences grade into each other so it is hard to say where one species—or race—ends and another begins.

The American marten may share its habitat with the fisher—a large, distinctive species weighing at least twice as much and therefore not a direct competitor for food and den sites. In Europe the range of the pine marten overlaps in the south with that of the stone marten or beech marten, while in the Far East lives the yellow-throated marten and its smaller Indian variant, the nilgiri marten.

MINKS

All these species have suffered at the hands of man, mainly because of their luxuriant fur. The dense winter pelts of the northern martens are especially prized, and the fur of the sable has an exalted status as a symbol of luxury. The very word "sable" tends to conjure up images of wealth and glamour rather than small carnivores foraging for prey in the northern forests, an unenviable distinction shared by another branch of the weasel family—the minks.

These mustelids evolved in North America, but a few migrants spread west into Eurasia via Alaska and Siberia during the last Ice Age, when the sea level was lower and the Bering Strait was a land bridge. Rising seas later flooded the Strait and isolated the American and Eurasian minks, so they developed into very slightly different species, which today show no inclination to interbreed.

The minks evolved to exploit wetland habitats, relying on their thick fur, lithe bodies, and partially webbed feet. Although they are not underwater specialists like the otters—their eyes cannot focus clearly underwater, whereas the otters have fully amphibious sight—they compensate by exploiting a much wider range of prey, both on land and in the water. This gives them the flexibility to switch to alternative food sources if they find themselves in competition with their more specialized relatives, or if their preferred prey becomes scarce. It has also equipped them to survive in a world where, increasingly, nothing can be relied upon forever. ■

THE MARTEN'S FAMILY TREE

Among mustelids, the martens are the best equipped for hunting in the forests. They possess neither the adaptation for burrow hunting shown by the weasels, nor the earth-moving muscle of the badgers, and they may represent a less-specialized type ancestral to both these forms. The minks are a semiaquatic variation on the polecat theme, and have been classified in the same genus.

FISHER
Martes pennanti
(MAR-tez pen-ANT-ee)

Biggest of all the martens— discounting the wolverine— the fisher is a stocky denizen of the North American forests, where it is the primary predator on the North American porcupine. Its luxuriant fur is only slightly less costly than that of the sable, and in the early 20th century it was eradicated from much of its range by overtrapping, coupled with deforestation. Today numbers are increasing thanks to reintroductions and legislation.

AMERICAN MINK
Mustela vison
(MUSS-tell-a VIE-zon)

EUROPEAN MINK

More closely allied to the polecats than the martens, the minks are semiaquatic hunters with thick, almost black fur. Although similar to an otter in body form, a mink is much smaller and has a slender, wedge-shaped face instead of the otter's broad, whiskered muzzle. The American mink is now widely distributed in Europe as well as America, and may have displaced the similar but smaller native European mink in some regions.

WEASELS

OTTERS

POLECATS

WEASEL FAMIL
(MUSTELIDS)

PINE MARTEN
Martes martes
(MAR-tez MAR-tez)

Biggest of the Eurasian martens, the pine marten has chocolate-brown fur, a bushy tail, and a one-piece, yellow-tinged white "bib" on its chest. Shy and retiring, it is rarely seen even where common. It is one of the few animals capable of thriving in conifer plantations, and in Britain increased conifer planting over the last half-century has allowed the pine marten to extend its range.

YELLOW-THROATED MARTEN
Martes flavigula
(MAR-tez flav-i-GOO-la)

This elusive animal is one of two yellow-throated species—or possibly races of the same species—found in southern Asia; uniquely for a marten its range extends as far south as the equator. Like the pine marten it hunts both in the trees and on the ground, but it rarely ventures out of dense forest.

Color illustrations Carol Roberts

WOLVERINES

BADGERS

SKUNKS

ⒶNCESTORS

THE SEA MINK

When Europeans first settled the Atlantic coast of North America, the shores of New England were home to a large species of mink with a relatively coarse pelt of dark, reddish brown fur. It lived among the boulders littering the rocky beaches, and fed on sea fish and shellfish, rather like an Atlantic version of the sea otter. Sadly, being so much larger than the American mink, its pelt was more valuable—despite its poorer quality—and by about 1880 the sea mink had been hunted to extinction.

B/W illustrations Ruth Grewcock

ANATOMY: THE PINE MARTEN

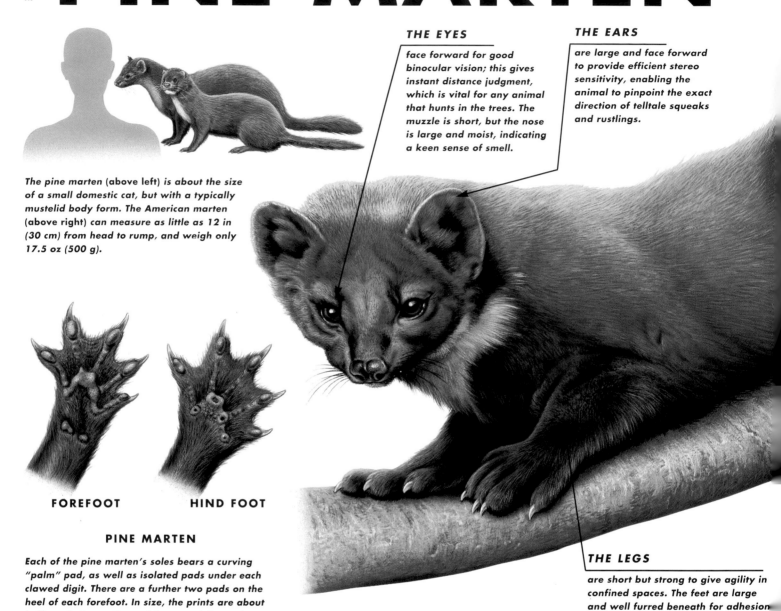

THE EYES

face forward for good binocular vision; this gives instant distance judgment, which is vital for any animal that hunts in the trees. The muzzle is short, but the nose is large and moist, indicating a keen sense of smell.

THE EARS

are large and face forward to provide efficient stereo sensitivity, enabling the animal to pinpoint the exact direction of telltale squeaks and rustlings.

The pine marten (above left) is about the size of a small domestic cat, but with a typically mustelid body form. The American marten (above right) can measure as little as 12 in (30 cm) from head to rump, and weigh only 17.5 oz (500 g).

FOREFOOT

HIND FOOT

PINE MARTEN

Each of the pine marten's soles bears a curving "palm" pad, as well as isolated pads under each clawed digit. There are a further two pads on the heel of each forefoot. In size, the prints are about halfway between those of foxes and domestic cats.

THE LEGS

are short but strong to give agility in confined spaces. The feet are large and well furred beneath for adhesion on snow, and have sharp claws to give a secure grip on tree bark.

The loosely articulated vertebrae of the marten's spine allow it to turn around in a confined space, or gallop at speed by arching and extending its back to provide a long stride. With the exception of the skull, the other bones are lightly built. The legs are short in relation to the cat-sized body, but the marten is not so "low-slung" as the stoat or weasel.

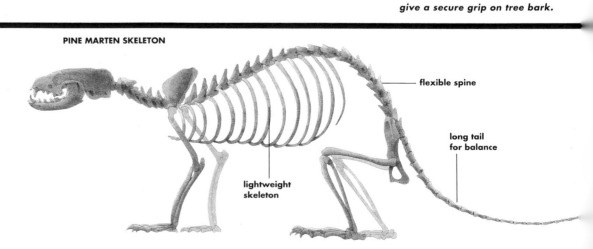

PINE MARTEN SKELETON

flexible spine

long tail for balance

lightweight skeleton

X-ray illustrations Elisabeth Smith

AMERICAN MINK

The mink's feet are slightly smaller than those of the pine marten. The five toes are widely splayed, and are partly webbed. The mink leaves copious tracks on muddy riverbanks, and the fine, star-shaped prints are the best proof of its identity.

FOREFOOT   **HIND FOOT**

PINE MARTEN

CLASSIFICATION

GENUS: *MARTES*
SPECIES: *MARTES*

SIZE

HEAD–BODY LENGTH: 16–23 IN (41–58 CM)
TAIL LENGTH: 8–11 IN (20–28 CM)
WEIGHT: 1.8–4.4 LB (0.8–2 KG)
WEIGHT AT BIRTH: 1 OZ (28 G)

COLORATION

CHOCOLATE-BROWN FUR WITH A WHITE, YELLOW-TINGED CHEST PATCH

FEATURES

LUXURIANT FUR
ELONGATED, SINUOUS BODY
SHORT LEGS
BUSHY TAIL

THE TAIL

is long and bushy, and acts as a rudder when the pine marten is leaping from branch to branch.

THE BODY

is long and sinuous, but more thickset than that of a weasel or polecat—although the bulky impression is largely due to the long, luxuriant fur for warmth in the northern winters. The pelt of the sable, the pine marten's closest relative, has always been considered the finest of all furs.

AMERICAN MARTEN SKULL

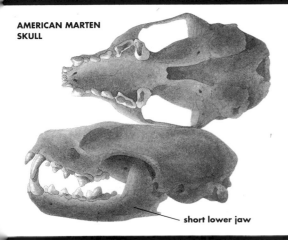

short lower jaw

The skull of a pine marten (right) is elongated, with a short lower jaw hinged well forward. This increases the leverage on the teeth, both for slicing meat with the scissorlike carnassial cheek teeth, and for delivering the fatal neck bite with the long, stabbing canines. Flattened molar teeth behind the carnassials enable the pine marten to chew fruit when it is seasonally abundant. The skull of the smaller American marten (left) has less prominent lower canines.

PINE MARTEN SKULL

carnassial teeth
canines

Main illustration Steve Kingston

CONFIDENT TRICKSTERS

MARTENS AND MINKS ARE EFFICIENT, VERSATILE CREATURES WITH THE ENTERPRISE AND AUDACITY TO MAKE THE MOST OF SITUATIONS WHERE HUMAN INFLUENCE DISCOURAGES THEIR LESS DARING COMPETITORS

Wayne Lankinen/Aquila

In 1979 there was a rash of car crimes in the Swiss town of Winterthur. For many months complaints of vandalism poured into the police offices, but the culprits were never found. One night, a patrolman parked his own car as bait and waited nearby. Hours later he watched, astonished, as a family of stone martens slipped into the engine bay and started to chew into the rubber coolant hoses and ignition cables.

This was no isolated incident. The habit spread, and by the end of the 1980s "martenized" cars were being reported throughout Switzerland, Austria, and Germany. The manufacturer Audi estimated that some 10,000 of its own customers' cars alone were being damaged each year, and now offers the option of a specially designed electric marten deterrent.

No one knows what attracts stone martens to the rubber hoses in car engines, but the sheer scale of their depredations is a measure of their enterprise in exploiting the urban environment. Martens have struck at cars in the heart of great cities like Munich, where flourishing populations of stone martens live rather like urban foxes—denning in cellars, attics, and outbuildings, and feeding on vermin and scraps when not indulging their taste for black rubber. The number of stone martens shot annually in Germany has risen tenfold since 1960—not because of some ruthless eradication campaign, but simply because they are that much more common in urban areas.

FINDING A NEW NICHE

The stone marten is unusually bold, but its adaptability is typical of martens in general. The pine marten can be equally flexible in its approach, and in some areas of Scotland where trapping in the past has eradicated polecat populations the martens have occupied the vacant niche, hunting entirely on the ground and denning in rock crevices and stone walls. Pine martens will readily move into the apparently sterile plantations of exotic conifers that have replaced the native forest over much of northern Europe, although only if they can find den sites. Perhaps other species, such as the sable, would discover similar inner resources if they were not so well suited to the vast forests of the Siberian taiga.

Compared to many of their relatives, martens are prepared to try a wide variety of plant and animal matter. This opportunist approach favors a solitary foraging style, since small prey is easily taken by a single, stealthy marten, but if a different strategy is required martens will adopt it. In the bleak, snowbound terrain of Arctic Scandinavia, for example, groups of martens will scavenge together in winter for the remains of large animals such as reindeer. Such feeding groups may be no more than

Manfred Danegger/NHPA

The rubber-chewing stone marten (above) *has adapted only too well to life in the big city.*

casual aggregations, but similar behavior among other carnivores (such as coyotes in North America) suggests that this may be a deliberate resource defense tactic, for several martens feeding together stand some chance of defending a reindeer carcass against a lynx or even a lone wolverine.

Mink are also resourceful, although they seem to be resolutely solitary. They are dedicated predators, with no taste for the scraps and gleanings that could sustain an urban stone marten. This means they find little to interest them in villages and towns, but they are adaptable enough to thrive in rural areas where human disturbance is frequent, provided there is adequate food. The American mink seems to be particularly bold, and is often easy to spot as it works a riverbank for prey. In the densely populated lowlands of Europe such confidence is a real asset, since it permits a mink to exploit habitats that other carnivores—and otters in particular—find untenable. Coupled with its willingness to experiment with prey, this is a formula for success in a world where human influence is almost inescapable. ∎

Martens are versatile hunter-foragers both on the ground and in the trees.

HABITATS

Although martens are adaptable enough to thrive in a wide variety of habitats, their strongholds lie in the great conifer belt of the north: the boreal forest, named after Boreas, the Greek god of the north wind, and known in Siberia as the taiga.

The taiga is the biggest forest in the world. In the former Soviet Union it stretches over 10,000 miles (over 16,000 km) from the Pacific to the Baltic, and extends west through Scandinavia to the shores of the North Atlantic. In North America, the forest covers much of Alaska and sprawls eastward across Canada to Labrador and Newfoundland. It is an immense ocean of trees, flanked to the south by the grassy steppes and prairies and to the north by the bleak, half-frozen swamplands of the Arctic tundra.

ALL-WEATHER MAMMALS

In the continental heart of the taiga the climate is testing in the extreme. In eastern Siberia the temperature may fall to –76°F (–60°C) in winter, yet in summer it may reach almost 100°F (38°C). There is little rain; even in wetter areas the rain often falls as snow and remains locked up as ice for much of the year. The conifers of the forest—pines, firs, spruces, and larches—are well equipped to survive these conditions, with tough, spiny leaves that resist water loss and drooping branches that shed snow before its weight builds up to timber-cracking levels, and they shield the animals of the forest from the worst weather. Even so, the animals need to be tough. The pine marten, the sable, and the fisher are among the

Mink rely on their coat of guard hairs and underfur to keep them warm.

Wayne Lankinen/Aquila

MINK AND OTTERS

In Britain the introduced American mink has been implicated in the decline of the native otter population. It is assumed that, as a semiaquatic hunter, the mink competes with the otter for food and territory, and has driven it out of its old haunts.

This is unlikely. At 22 lb (10 kg) the otter is ten times the size of the 2.2 lb (1 kg) mink, and accordingly it concentrates on much larger prey. Otters studied in Scandinavia fed mainly on large fish, while mink living alongside them preyed on small mammals such as water voles. Both will catch small fish and frogs, but as an underwater specialist the otter is more likely to take them in deep water while the mink scoops them out of the shallows. Mink tend to prefer overgrown waterways that are unsuitable for the otter's underwater hunting technique. Where the two occur together they can usually live in harmony, for an otter will have no objection to an animal of a different species occupying part of its territory.

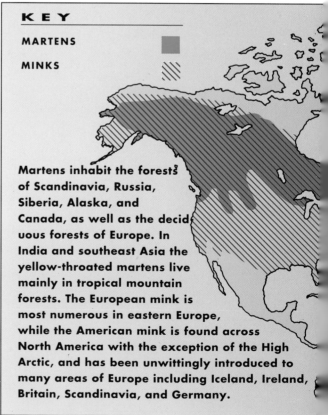

KEY

MARTENS

MINKS

Martens inhabit the forests of Scandinavia, Russia, Siberia, Alaska, and Canada, as well as the deciduous forests of Europe. In India and southeast Asia the yellow-throated martens live mainly in tropical mountain forests. The European mink is most numerous in eastern Europe, while the American mink is found across North America with the exception of the High Arctic, and has been unwittingly introduced to many areas of Europe including Iceland, Ireland, Britain, Scandinavia, and Germany.

toughest, thanks to the superb insulation provided by their legendary silky fur. The fur comprises two distinct layers: Long guard hairs cast off the rain and protect against physical damage, and a denser underfur retains an insulating blanket of air around the animal's body core. In spring much of the fur is molted to leave a shorter, coarser summer coat, but in autumn the thick pelt grows again to see the animal through the winter.

Although quite capable of bearing the Arctic cold, martens rarely stray north of the tree line into the tundra zone, even in summer when prey is abundant on the grasslands. They are forest-hunters, and although species like the sable and the fisher hunt mainly on the ground, rather than in the forest canopy, they rely on the trees to provide cover—both for them and for their prey. To the south they readily colonize deciduous forest, and in western Ireland, for example, pine martens flourish in the hazel woodlands of County Clare. In Britain they were common in the oak woodlands of southern England as recently as the mid-18th century, and there are records of martens being trapped in woodland near Arundel, near the south coast, in the 1840s. Their disappearance from such regions had more to do with persecution than a preference for more rigorous habitats, and today pine martens still flourish in the deciduous forests of France, Germany, and central Europe, occurring as far south as Sicily.

Richard Day/Oxford Scientific Films

A fisher eating a rare meal of fish. This species is better known for its prowess in penetrating the spiny defenses of the North American porcupine.

In general the pine marten seems to prefer scrub woodland with plenty of fruit-bearing bushes, abundant prey, and good ground cover; it is rarely seen in the open, and even individuals that live on heather moors take care to stay out of sight. Martens do not have many enemies apart from humans, but they are regularly caught and eaten by eagles, the only birds of prey that are powerful enough to carry them aloft. Wolves may take them, but the strong smell of their scent glands—although not unpleasant to us—tends

DISTRIBUTION

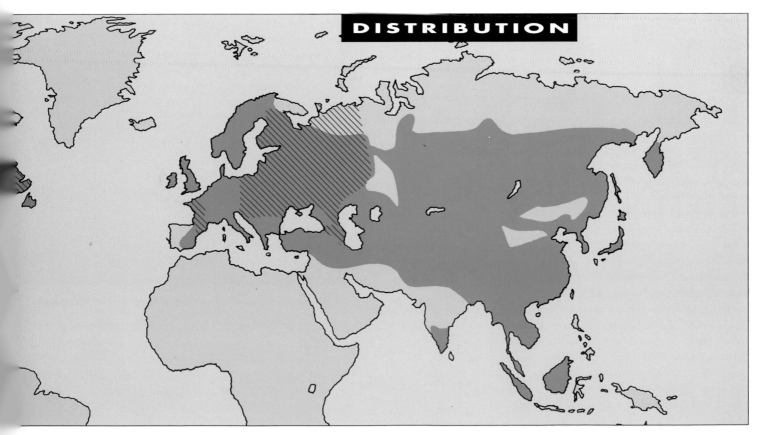

to discourage all but the most determined mammal predator. Since birds cannot smell, eagles are not deterred in the same way.

Most habitats support only one marten species at a time. In the forests of North America, however, the fisher may share territory with the American marten. This works because the bigger, more powerful fisher tends to concentrate on prey that the smaller marten could not tackle. The size difference also means there is no competition for den sites, for the American marten can squeeze into crevices that the fisher would not consider.

In Europe a similar size differential reduces the potential rivalry between the introduced American mink and the Eurasian otter (see box, page 1312) but there is little difference between the newcomer and the native European mink, which occupies exactly the same ecological niche. Consequently it is feared that the now-rare European species has been displaced by its more vigorous cousin in some regions. In others, however, such as Britain, the absence of the European species left the niche vacant, and the American mink simply filled it.

Both species of mink commonly live along riverbanks and in reedbeds, swamps, and marshes; like martens, they like to keep close to cover. In winter mink may abandon their summer hunting grounds if

Manfred Danegger/NHPA

FOCUS ON

CALEDONIAN FOREST

Some 2,000 years ago the great boreal forests extended across Europe to northern Britain. The ancient Caledonian forest has now largely disappeared from Scotland, its place taken by heather moorland. The fragments that remain are the strongholds of the pine marten in Britain.

The dominant tree in these primeval woodlands is the Scots pine, one of only three species of conifer native to Britain. Scots pine is a common tree on acid soils throughout Britain, but it achieves a particular majesty in the Caledonian forest. The trees provide food for a variety of birds, such as the goldcrest, siskin, crested tit, and crossbill, as well as the red squirrel—all potential prey for the pine marten and the sparrow hawks, kestrels, and buzzards that patrol the skies. The surrounding scrub of heather, bilberry, and bracken provides cover for gamebirds such as the blackcock and the mighty capercaillie, red and roe deer, and small mammals and the carnivores that stalk them such as the red fox, weasel, marten, and, in some areas, the wildcat. In the valleys there may be otters fishing the clear waters of the Highland rivers, adding a finishing touch to a scene that, in these fragments of ancient forest, has barely changed since the end of the Ice Age.

TEMPERATURE AND RAINFALL

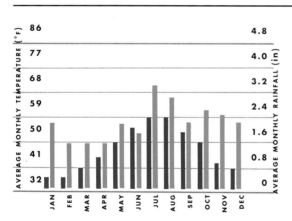

■ TEMPERATURE

■ RAINFALL

Winter brings frosts and deep snowfalls, obliging all but the hardiest birds and mammals to migrate or hibernate. The summer is mild and moist, and, in typical Scottish style, heavy rains persist through the autumn.

the water freezes over and move on to fast-flowing streams where the water moves too rapidly for ice to form. This may involve moving uphill, unlike most other animals which tend to move downhill into the valleys in winter to take advantage of the milder climate. Such considerations are irrelevant to a mink, for like the sable it has a luxuriant fur coat with up to twenty-four underfur hairs for each guard hair. The American mink thrives as far north as northern Alaska, and the European mink may hunt over the tundra on the icy coast of the Arctic Ocean. ■

NEIGHBORS

Some of Britain's rarest mammals can still be found in the cool, fragrant glades of the Caledonian forest, while the pine seeds provide a rich source of food for the many birds.

WILDCAT

The wildcat looks like a domestic cat but for its more massive head, thick coat, and bushy, blunt tail.

CROSSBILL

The crossbill uses its bizarre beak and thick, leathery tongue to snip out and eat the seeds from pine cones.

Neighbor illustrations Ruth Grewcock. Crossbill and moth Andrew Robinson/Wildlife Art Agency

CALEDONIAN PINES

Naturally regenerated from strewn seeds, Scots pine trees are broadly spaced like oaks in an English woodland, and grow to a similar size. The remaining stands of Caledonian forest are scattered throughout the Highlands and along the valleys of rivers such as the Spey.

■ **ANCIENT FOREST**

RED DEER

This deer is widespread in Britain, but its strongholds lie among the Grampians and Highlands of Scotland.

WOOD ANT

These ants forage along paths up to 100 ft (30 m) from their nests among the fallen pine needles.

RED FOX

Now common in our cities and suburbs, the red fox preys upon the voles and rabbits of the pine forest.

CAPERCAILLIE

Now sadly rare, the magnificent capercaillie cock lures his mate with a raucous, thrilling call.

PINE BEAUTY MOTH

This moth blends well with the bark of pine trunks, and its caterpillars look rather like pine needles.

HUNTING

Like the distant ancestors of all mustelids, the martens are built for hunting in the trees, and no other carnivore can match them for agility in the forest canopy. A pine marten in full cry will career up a tree trunk and along a branch with breathtaking speed, leaping from tree to tree with an apparently reckless disregard for its own safety. Occasionally it falls, but its light weight, thick fur, and acrobatic instinct usually insure that it suffers no harm. Pine martens have been seen to fall from heights of up to 65 ft (20 m) and simply carry on with the hunt.

A pine marten—the most arboreal species—will take a wide variety of prey in the trees. In spring and summer fledglings and eggs are easy targets, and the marten is often quick enough to catch the parent birds before they can escape. Its slender build enables it to penetrate tortuous crevices in search of tasty morsels, and it will readily take beetles, other insects, and larvae if the opportunity presents itself.

> A MARTEN WAS ONCE SEEN KNOCKING BUMBLEBEES DOWN ONE AFTER ANOTHER WITH A FOREPAW AND EATING THEM BEFORE THEY COULD RECOVER

The pine marten's speciality, however, is hunting squirrels. Among martens studied in the forests of Sweden, squirrels accounted for 51 percent of the diet, with the remainder made up of 21 percent other small mammals, 18 percent birds, and 10 percent fruit, insects, and other items. The percentages vary from time to time, depending on the relative abundance of the various types of prey, but squirrels always figure heavily. Some 10 percent of Swedish red squirrels are taken by martens each winter.

Apart from birds of prey such as the goshawk, which plucks squirrels off the branches with its long talons, they have no other key predator in the trees. Accordingly evolution has tailored the marten to make the most of its opportunity, and it can pursue a fleeing squirrel wherever it goes, with one exception: It cannot follow the much-lighter squirrel out to the slender outer twigs of a tree—and the squirrel knows it. In such circumstances cunning takes over from sheer speed and agility, and the pursuing marten may outflank the squirrel and panic it into making a leap for another branch or tree. This is the marten's cue to strike, and it will often leap up to

Pine martens seem to follow one simple rule with regard to the scope of their diet: If it moves, eat it!

DYNAMIC DUELS
The agility of the pine marten so closely mirrors that of a squirrel that the two almost appear to have been designed in tandem, operating in a deadly partnership of predator and prey.

Tony Stone Worldwide

Illustrations Kim Thompson

YOUNG VICTIMS

However fiercely a bird protects its clutch, a few fatalities are to be expected. Some chicks fall prey to other birds, such as raptors, jays, or crows, while others— and even the parents— are snapped up by the pine marten (right).

snatch the squirrel in midair, seizing it in its claws and falling to the ground. There it rolls over to pinion the squirrel and deliver a fatal bite to the throat or the back of the neck with its long, sharp canines.

In the north squirrels often migrate in autumn to find good sources of food, which are vital if they are to build up their energy reserves sufficiently to survive the winter. Such is the dependence of martens on squirrels that they, too, may migrate, following the squirrels rather as wolves will trail herds of reindeer through the snow on the forest floor below.

Over most of its range the pine marten hunts mainly in the trees, but in Britain, possibly because of long-term deforestation, the pine marten forages widely on the ground. Squirrels are still a favored prey, but it also consumes a lot of small rodents, particularly voles. It eats a lot of fruit when available; a bramble bush with a rich crop of blackberries will keep a marten occupied every night for a week.

On the ground the marten follows a zigzag course as it combs the terrain for likely prey refuges, dashing in pursuit of any animals it flushes from cover. Owing to its short stature it often loses sight of its prey and has to track it by scent, pausing occasionally to rear up on its hind legs and scan all around. Other martens employ a similar ground-hunting technique: The sable in particular forages mainly at ground level in the Siberian forests, and

1317

the stone marten is skilled at tracking prey in rocky terrain. The most remarkable ground-hunting technique, however, has been developed by the fisher.

THE FISHER TECHNIQUE

Fishers are big animals—a male can weigh 13 lb (6 kg) or more—and they need plenty of food. A big male may have to catch the equivalent of twenty voles a day, which is hard work. A couple of squirrels would do as well, and fishers often hunt in the trees like the smaller martens, although with less agility. Ideally they go for the kind of big, meaty prey that makes a long hunt worthwhile: Hares are favored targets, but the real speciality of the fisher is the North American porcupine.

Many predators would make a meal of a porcupine if they could, for at up to 40 lb (18 kg) it is a rich prize. But few can get past the potentially lethal quills. The fisher manages it because, with its short mustelid legs, its teeth are down on a level with the porcupine's face. It baits its quarry, then nips in to bite it on the nose. If it manages to score five or six good hits the porcupine is likely to succumb from blood loss and shock, allowing the fisher to flip it over on its back and get at its soft underbelly. The kill may take half an hour or more to achieve, but the effort is well worth it since, scavengers permitting, the fisher may have secured enough meat to last it ten days or more.

Despite its name the fisher very rarely catches fish; it leaves such slippery prey to the mink. Lacking the specialized underwater equipment of the otters, a mink tends to hunt fish from the surface, watching the water from the bank or a convenient rock and diving in to snatch any fish that swim within range. It also hunts crayfish and crabs underwater but has difficulty pursuing fast-swimming prey owing to its air-adapted eyesight. It prefers to hunt in the shallows, or on the matted vegetation of swamps and reedbeds, taking frogs, water voles, muskrats, and waterfowl. It will also pursue and kill rabbits, rats,

Crawfish scuttling slowly in the shallows of a riverbed present a fairly easy target to the dexterous paws and super-fast reactions of a mink (above).

Claude Steelman/Survival Anglia

FAST FOOD

Fish and eels usually prove too elusive for a mink, although it will have a go all the same (left). Such speedy prey is best left to the fully amphibious otter.

PRICKLY PREY

A porcupine at bay will usually turn its back to a predator and lash out with its tail (below left). The fisher, however, has a knack of baiting the porcupine into turning about and exposing its vulnerable face.

and other land animals, using its well-developed sense of smell to track them down and even follow them into their burrows.

Mink take a much broader range of prey than otters, switching from one food source to another as season and opportunity dictate. They are resourceful animals with a talent for getting through fences and other barriers, and they often break into fish farms, game-rearing pens, and chicken runs. In these circumstances mink can become mesmerized by the sight of so much prey, and may kill everything in sight. This phenomenon, known as surplus killing, results from the fact that the prey cannot escape as it would in the wild, so the mink's instinct to kill is triggered over and over again until it is exhausted.

Under normal conditions any surplus food is cached for later use, since a predator can never be sure of its next meal, and this instinct to kill and hoard is almost certainly the origin of surplus killing. One mink den was found to contain two mallard ducks, a coot, and thirteen muskrats, all freshly killed in what must have been a profitable hunting spree. For despite their opportunist habits and lack of specialized hunting adaptations, mink are efficient killers, capable of making a profound impact on any ecosystem they invade. On some offshore islands escaped mink have decimated colonies of ground-nesting seabirds which were previously safe from ground predators, and since there is no sure way of preventing their escape several applications to start fur farms on island sites have been bluntly turned down. ∎

in SIGHT

A PEST UNCHECKED

Now one of the most familiar of British mammals, the gray squirrel originated from the hardwood forests of the eastern United States. It was introduced to Britain in 1876 as a picturesque addition to the fauna, but it soon began to breed rapidly and, owing to bark-stripping habits, has become a woodland pest. In its native America its numbers were kept under control by local predators, but in Britain it has only one serious enemy—the pine marten. Unfortunately pine martens had virtually disappeared from the English lowlands by the time the gray squirrel arrived, so the squirrel multiplies virtually unchecked.

Ironically the last strongholds of the pine marten in Britain are also refuges for the threatened red squirrel, which could well do without such an enemy.

Illustrations Brian Edwards/Wildlife Art Agency

TERRITORY

Minks and martens normally avoid company outside the mating season and, although a young family may hunt together with their mother to learn their trade, they soon go solo, dispersing to find hunting grounds of their own which they claim as territories.

A territory is a valuable asset to a mink or a marten, but to a mink in particular. Although minks occasionally eat insects, earthworms, and other prey that may be temporarily abundant, they concentrate on small vertebrates such as waterfowl, voles, frogs, and fish. These are generally more scarce and harder to catch, but the supply is usually steady from day to day, and in any particular region a mink can satisfy its needs for much of the year by staying within a well-defined area—a home range.

If it shares this range with another mink the area will need to be that much bigger to satisfy the food requirements of both. While this may be acceptable up to a point—in the interests of securing a mate— the extra energy used by foraging over a wider area for the same result makes it undesirable. A breeding female in particular needs to conserve her energy if she is to produce enough milk for her young, so she has every reason to stay close to home. Her best

chance of insuring a supply of prey is to discourage neighboring mink—females in particular—from poaching on her patch, so she defends it as an exclusive territory.

In general the richer the habitat, the smaller and more stable the territories. In really poor habitats mink may be forced to wander nomadically to find enough prey. In the Arctic martens do the same, sometimes gathering together to scavenge large carcasses. In such circumstances the territorial instinct seems to be shelved. Where prey is abundant, however, the territories are small, easily defended, and therefore well defined. In the case of mink they tend to take the form of elongated strips of marshland or riverbank, some 0.6–2.5 mi (1–4 km) long, with several dens located near the water. Marten territories tend to be bigger: Where a mink territory in marshland rarely covers more than 22 acres (9 hectares), a pine marten territory may extend over 62 acres

WATERSIDE RANGE

A stretch of riverbank usually provides a solitary mink with all the bare necessities— enough birds, fish, and frogs to eat, and thickets of ground cover (right).

Illustration Robin Budden/Wildlife Art Agency

Mary Clay/Planet Earth Pictures

Martens actively defend their woodland territories to secure their hunting rights.

(25 hectares) of woodland, although it may be smaller where prey is abundant. A small territory is regularly patrolled on a daily basis; larger territories have "core areas" that are used more intensively, but the resident will still do its best to exclude intruders from the whole area.

SCENT MARKING

Territories are defined by scent marks, using the pungent musk secreted by the anal glands as well as more subtle scents produced by glands on the throat and chest. These secretions are often smeared directly on prominent landmarks, but the anal gland musk is also used to anoint the animal's scats (feces) which are deposited in conspicuous places to warn off trespassers. Pine martens leave theirs on rocks, logs, ant hills, and the tops of stone walls, as well as by the sides of well-worn paths that have often been used by martens for generations. Experienced naturalists can identify these scats by their smell: Those

SCENT DEPOSITS

warn other minks away (right). *They are clear in their meaning and resolve potential conflicts peacefully.*

of minks tend to smell fishy while the musk on a pine marten scat bears an unlikely resemblance to the smell of violets.

To the animals concerned, the smell of a scat may communicate quite complex information, indicating the diet, sex, sexual condition, health, and even identity of the animal that deposited it. Quite possibly, on a subconscious level,

SCENT AND SOLITUDE

All carnivores use scent for communication, but it is particularly important to species that normally lead solitary lives since it enables information to be broadcast without involving visual contact. Such scent signals are far too subtle for our own poor senses to appreciate, and may be more complex than we imagine.

For example, although they are mainly solitary, small mustelids establish social hierarchies and dominant stoats are known to scent mark more often than low-ranking stoats. This may simply reflect their greater confidence, but it is likely that a stoat can actually smell the difference in status, possibly because of varying levels of sex hormone in the scent cocktail. The same probably applies to martens and minks, allowing the animals to advertise their superiority without resorting to energy-sapping physical confrontations.

encountering another individual's scent tends to undermine an intruder's confidence, making it easier for the resident to drive it away; but if the scent mark conveys evidence of weakness through age or ill health, the intruder may be tempted to push its luck and extend its own territory.

Obviously sexual information is of paramount interest to males actively searching for mates, and in some populations of minks and fishers a male will establish a large territory superimposed on those of several females and attempt to mate with them all. His intention may be thwarted, however, by invading rival males attracted by the females' scent marks. Alternatively the breeding season may inspire males to abandon their feeding territories and range far afield in search of receptive females. The choice of strategy seems to vary from area to area, and may depend on the richness of the habitat. The richer it is, the smaller the female territories and the closer together they are, making them easier to control by a resident male. Either way it helps if the male is big and powerful, and among both martens and minks the male is substantially bigger than the female. A mature male fisher weighs twice as much as his sister, giving him the power to face up to rivals and the motivation to range widely in search of the prey he needs to sustain his bulk. This in turn brings him into contact with more females, yet reduces competition with them because, being bigger, he tends to hunt larger prey. ■

LIFE CYCLE

Mating can be a rough business for a female marten or mink. Being so much smaller than the male she is in no position to resist his advances, and any attempt to do so would be painful and possibly dangerous. A rutting male grabs his intended by the scruff of her neck, often drawing blood with his teeth; she bears the mark forever in the form of a patch of white hair growing on the scar tissue.

This may seem like senseless violence, but it has its purpose. In these animals ovulation—the release of the unfertilized eggs from the female's ovaries—is triggered by the mating act. This is a virtual guarantee of conception, provided the trigger operates. To be certain of this, the female has to undergo a traumatic mating ritual which not only leaves her scarred for life but also insures that her reproductive system is given the necessary kick start.

ROUGHNECKS
A sore neck is also the male's way of forcing the female to submit while he mounts her; some force is needed because copulation may last for up to three hours, with plenty of purring and growling. Eventually the male flags, releases the female, and, having recuperated, sets off in search of another. He will try to mate with as many females as possible each season, attempting to secure his genetic future by the sheer number of his offspring rather than by helping rear them to insure their survival.

MATING

is a rough affair, and the male subdues his mate forcibly by biting her neck (above).

SEXUAL MATURITY

is reached at just over two years. By this stage the youngsters are fully independent and capable of catching their own prey (left).

Despite her rough handling the female is also likely to mate again. American mink are interesting in this respect, since the female has four receptive periods. She may mate with several males during each of these periods, and then will bear a mixed litter of young sired by different fathers. The males who mate with her toward the end of the season tend to sire more of her kits. Since only the strongest males keep going until the end of the season the late matings tend to produce young sired by the strongest males, but if all the males in the neighborhood have dropped out through exhaustion the female will bear a litter anyway, from an earlier mating.

Mink babies are helpless and sightless until almost four weeks old.

Erwin & Peggy Bauer/Bruce Coleman Ltd.

GROWING UP

The life of a young sable

Some male mink generate more young than females. Although both sexes mate promiscuously, a female can only bear one litter each season, while a male has the potential to sire four or more. Selective advantage for any animal is played out by producing as many descendants as possible. It could pay a female to give birth to sons rather than daughters to maximise the potential number of grandchildren but only if her sons are highly competitive. Less vigorous sons may have no offspring at all. Some data suggest that the healthiest, well-fed young females will conceive and rear more vigorous males. Females in less than optimal condition appear to conceive more daughters. In both cases, the mothers have optimized their chances for the most grandchildren.

THE LITTER

is born in a hollow log or a den. There are up to four blind, deaf, and helpless babies (above).

PRANKSTERS

At fifty to sixty days old the young sables are confident enough to venture from the den. They indulge in lively play-fights (above).

FROM BIRTH TO DEATH

MINK
GESTATION: 27–33 DAYS, PLUS UP TO 30-DAY DELAYED IMPLANTATION
LITTER SIZE: 4–6
BREEDING: MATE IN EARLY SPRING, GIVE BIRTH EARLY SUMMER
EYES OPEN: 25 DAYS
WEANING: 8–10 WEEKS
FIRST LEAVE DEN: 8 WEEKS
INDEPENDENCE: 3–4 MONTHS
SEXUAL MATURITY: 10 MONTHS
LONGEVITY: 10 YEARS OR MORE IN THE WILD

PINE MARTEN
GESTATION: 60 DAYS PLUS UP TO 6-MONTH DELAYED IMPLANTATION
LITTER SIZE: 2–4
BREEDING: MATE IN LATE SUMMER, GIVE BIRTH EARLY SPRING
EYES OPEN: 35 DAYS
WEANING: ABOUT 8 WEEKS
FIRST LEAVE DEN: 8 WEEKS
INDEPENDENCE: 3–4 MONTHS
SEXUAL MATURITY: 2 YEARS
LONGEVITY: 15 YEARS OR MORE IN THE WILD

Illustrations Joanne Cowne

A long pregnancy follows, for although the gestation period for young mink is some thirty days, they are not simply born a month after conception. If they were, they would be launched into the world in autumn, when the mother needs all her energies to weather the winter; they would also have to endure the winter cold themselves and might not survive. Accordingly the birth is postponed by putting the system on hold. Instead of immediately becoming implanted in the wall of the womb and developing into an embryo, the fertilized egg—or blastocyst—floats in suspended animation for several months. Eventually the blastocyst implants and develops a placenta, and the pregnancy proceeds as normal. In mink this delays the birth by up to two months, so the pregnancy may last three times as long as the actual gestation. But the record for delayed implantation goes to the fisher, which mates in early spring and extends its two-month "true" gestation by some nine months to give an eleven-month pregnancy—as long as that of the blue whale.

In pine martens the two to six kits are born in early spring in a den among stones, in a hollow tree or cave, or even in a pirated bird's nest. They are born blind, deaf, and sparsely furred, and develop relatively slowly. Although weaned at about six weeks they stay in the nursery den until they are at least two months old. Once they are mobile they play together for hours at a time, wrestling and mock fighting. They start to grow fast on solid food, reaching adult weight at about three months old. By this stage they are hunting with their mother and are able to kill prey, but they stay with her for another three months before leaving to fend for themselves at the end of summer. ∎

FABLED FURS

FOR CENTURIES THE MARTENS AND MINKS HAVE SUFFERED THROUGH EXPLOITATION FOR THEIR VALUABLE FUR, BUT TODAY THEIR FUTURES ARE JEOPARDIZED MAINLY BY DEFORESTATION AND POLLUTION

I n the late 18th century the Siberian city of Irbit was the sable capital of the world. Each year, several hundred thousand sable pelts were traded with the merchants who crossed the Urals from European Russia to do business with the fur trappers. A huge amount of money changed hands—for then, as now, the sable was one of the most valuable of all furs. Luxurious in the extreme, it was prized throughout Europe as a symbol of wealth and status, and when the supply began to dwindle the traders simply paid more for rarity value. By 1910 the number of pelts traded annually at Irbit had slumped to around 20,000, and throughout vast areas of Siberia the sable was in serious trouble.

This might seem inevitable, but similar exploitation of the ermine, or stoat, had caused no such crisis: It was a fast breeder, able to recover rapidly from population crashes caused by regular prey famines on the Arctic tundra. The sable and the other martens do not share this bounce-back capacity, for they are used to a stable habitat where prey famines are rare. Each animal could expect to live fifteen years or more, so it could afford to breed relatively slowly by producing a litter of two to four young each season, as opposed to the short-lived ermine's brood of up to twelve. Small wonder, then, that intensive trapping set the sable on the road to extinction while barely affecting its smaller relative.

GOOD NEWS FOR PORCUPINES

In North America the fisher suffered a similar decline for the same reasons. Its pelt lacks the mystique of the sable, but it can be almost as fine and it is much larger. The effects of trapping throughout the 19th and early 20th centuries were compounded by habitat destruction through logging, and by the 1920s the fisher had almost disappeared from the United States and much of eastern Canada.

This decline had an unexpected consequence. The fisher is the only effective predator of porcupines in the northern forests, so in its absence the porcupines thrived. Porcupines have a habit of stripping bark for food, which kills trees, and as their numbers rose the rate of destruction in new plantations accelerated. Eventually the role of the fisher in preventing this was recognized, and the 1930s saw the introduction of closed seasons and other controls on trapping and hunting. During the 1950s and 1960s fishers were reintroduced to various forests in the United States, where the species is now flourishing.

Back in Siberia the sable's decline had become a major issue, and the species became the subject of a research program and a number of control measures, including trapping quotas and closed seasons.

H. Chr. Lohmann/Okapia/Oxford Scientific Films

The trade in mink pelts relies mainly today upon stocks from captive-breeding fur farms (above).

S. Maslowski/Frank Lane Picture Agency

This map shows the former and current distributional range of the European mink.

FORMER
DISTRIBUTION

CURRENT
DISTRIBUTION

Competition with the very similar American mink has probably contributed to the rarity of the European mink. It was once common and widespread over Europe, from northern Spain and France to Siberia. Today it is rare in central Europe, where feral American minks thrive in large numbers, having escaped from fur farms. Water pollution is another contributory factor in its decline.

As with the fisher, the policy seems to be working and wild sable populations are apparently increasing. The animal is also farmed for its fur, and fur-farmed sable accounts for about 10 percent of the pelts traded annually.

Fur farming has played a far more substantial part in the mink trade. The first mink "fur farms" were established way back in 1866, and today most of the mink pelts used by furriers are from fur-farmed stock; this has relieved the pressure on wild populations. Fur farming has also affected the distribution of wild mink, since, owing to the higher quality of its pelt—compared with the European mink—the American species has been used to stock all the fur farms established in Europe. The inevitable escapees have thrived and multiplied in

The American mink is larger than its European cousin and more adaptable to new surroundings.

1325

ALONGSIDE MAN

PASTEL MINK

American minks have been bred on fur farms since 1866, partly as an easy option compared to fur trapping, but partly also because controlled breeding permits selection for qualities such as size and color. Most of the mink bred in captivity are in fact hybrids between the dark Labrador race and the large Alaskan race, yielding an animal that is both big and richly colored, but several color varieties have been produced by careful inbreeding of mutant strains. These include white, black, and a range of pale shades with fanciful names such as platinum, silver, and sapphire. Occasionally such "pastel mink" turn up in the wild, but they are nearly always recent escapees from captivity since the normal color has a selective advantage and usually overwhelms the human-selected colors within a few generations.

Tony Bomford/Oxford Scientific Films

their new surroundings, and today there are flourishing wild populations of American mink in Britain, Ireland, Iceland, Scandinavia, Russia, and Germany. The invaders are blamed for driving Eurasian otters away from their former habitats, as well as destroying valuable game fish, raiding henhouses, killing gamebirds, and other delinquencies. Much of this is prejudice, but the animal is widely regarded as vermin and treated accordingly—an odd state of affairs considering the value of its fur as a status symbol.

Meanwhile the European mink has become rare, and competition with the introduced American mink may be a factor in this. It has also been heavily trapped for its fur and as a threat to poultry and

In the mid-1980s, a sable pelt was worth $500 on the world market. Trade still continues, despite the huge swing in public opinion against the wearing of fur coats.

other domestic stock, but the real reasons for its decline are probably less direct. Across its range wetlands have suffered badly from drainage, canalization, and hydroelectric schemes, as well as the appalling pollution that has poisoned the rivers and landscape in so much of eastern Europe.

The sable, fisher, and mink may yield some of the most valuable furs, but the other marten species have also been heavily exploited. The pine marten, Japanese marten, and American marten have all been excessively trapped for their luxuriant fur, and wild populations have suffered accordingly. The stone martens and the yellow-throated martens of the Far East have relatively poor-quality pelts and have been largely ignored by the trappers; even so, the Taiwan race of the yellow-throated marten and the south Indian nilgiri marten have become very rare, largely as a result of habitat erosion.

The pine marten has also been badly affected by deforestation in Europe, although the creation of new plantations in recent decades may be reversing this trend. The only species that seems to flourish regardless of human activity is the stone marten, which scores through its preference for rocky, barren areas and a notorious willingness to colonize urban environments and exploit human artifacts. Is it possible that its enthusiasm for vandalizing cars is inspired by more than a taste for chewing black rubber? Perhaps, on behalf of all its relatives who have been evicted from their forests or turned into fur coats, the stone marten is fighting back. ∎

MARTENS AND MINKS IN DANGER

THE CHART BELOW SHOWS HOW, IN 1994, THE INTERNATIONAL UNION FOR THE CONSERVATION OF NATURE (IUCN), OR THE WORLD CONSERVATION UNION, CLASSIFIED THE CONSERVATION STATUS OF THE MARTENS AND MINKS THAT ARE KNOWN OR SUSPECTED TO BE UNDER SERIOUS THREAT:

EUROPEAN MINK	**ENDANGERED**
NILGIRI MARTEN	**VULNERABLE**

ENDANGERED MEANS THAT THE SPECIES IS FACING A VERY HIGH PROBABILITY OF EXTINCTION IN THE NEAR FUTURE. *VULNERABLE* MEANS THAT THE SPECIES IS LIKELY TO DECLINE AND BECOME ENDANGERED IF NOTHING IS DONE TO IMPROVE ITS SITUATION.

INTO THE FUTURE

If the erosion of their habitats can be slowed down, the martens and minks—the American mink, at any rate—may have the versatility to recover from the low ebb to which they were brought by uncontrolled fur trapping in the past. Compared with many of their relatives in the weasel family they are relatively unspecialized animals with an opportunist instinct that encourages them to investigate and exploit unfamiliar environments. The stone marten is the most adventurous in this respect, rivaling the

PREDICTION

THE MINK DIFFERENCE

While populations of the European mink continue to dwindle, the American mink is expanding its range in Britain, Iceland, Scandinavia, and Russia. If the current trend continues it may well spread throughout Europe.

red fox in its willingness to colonize improbable habitats, but the pine marten has also shown itself capable of thriving in conditions that would have been quite alien to its forest-dwelling ancestors.

In parts of northwest Scotland the pine marten prospers on open hillsides, including scree slopes, and thriving populations also live among the cliffs, crags, and boulders of rocky shores. This is traditional polecat terrain, and it is possible that the pine marten has simply occupied a niche left vacant by the local extinction of the polecat in Scotland. Whether or not this is so, the pine marten's ability to exploit the opportunity is encouraging proof of its adaptability, and since the other northern martens are more or less identical in all respects other than size, they may be equally versatile.

These martens have certainly responded well to human help. Reintroduced during the 1950s and 1960s, the fisher has flourished in the United States, going from a condition of near extinction to the point where there are viable populations in at least fourteen states. The much-smaller American marten has also made something of a comeback. ■

THE BAIKAL SABLES

Owing to its value as a fur-bearing animal the sable has been afforded a degree of protection ever since the 17th century, when the felling of trees in the sable grounds of Siberia was prohibited by Czar Peter the Great. Some of the most prized sable pelts come from the pine forests to the east of Lake Baikal, and in 1916, following a dramatic fall in sable numbers, a nature preserve was created at Barguzin on the lake's northeastern shores.

Occupying an area of 1,016 sq miles (2,631 sq km), the preserve stretches along nearly 60 miles (97 km) of the Baikal shore. It acts as a refuge for thirty-nine mammal species, including the Baikal seal, a landlocked race of the ringed seal that is unique to this area. Today there is increasing concern over water pollution in the lake itself, depite its immense volume. However, the Barguzin reserve—although initially set up to conserve a valuable economic resource—now provides a safe haven for the sable which has responded by building up a healthy local population of close to three animals for every square mile of protected forest.

THE FUR TRADE

The fisher and American marten are still trapped for their fur, as are their Eurasian counterparts; over 100,000 American martens are trapped each season, and although the kill is restricted by law a slow-breeding species cannot easily sustain such heavy mortality. Luckily the campaign against the exploitation of fur-bearing animals appears to be having some effect, and if the market for furs continues to contract at the current rate the trappers may have to find other ways of earning a living.

Illustration Evi Antoniou

MEERKATS

RELATIONS

Meerkats and other mongooses belong to the Viverrid family, Viverridae. Other members of this family include:

CIVETS

GENETS

LINSANGS

FALANOUC

FOSSA

FANALOKA

David Macdonald/Oxford Scientific Films

SMALL AND FEARLESS

MONGOOSES ARE INDUSTRIOUS FORAGERS OF INSECTS BUT ARE FEARLESS WHEN CONFRONTED BY THEIR MUCH LARGER ENEMIES

eerkats are weasel-like creatures that live in Africa, Asia, and parts of southern Europe. They belong to the mongoose family—itself part of the Viverridae family—which also includes genets, civets, and linsangs. These animals are all very different in appearance from mongooses.

Mongooses' legs are short and their bodies long; they have pointed snouts and small rounded ears on the sides of their head. In some species, the eyes

are prominent. Their tails are long and sometimes bushy; their feet have four or five toes and some species use their hands to hold food while they are eating. They are commonly divided into two types—solitary and pack living, or social.

The Viverridae family has its origins in the ancestor of all carnivores, the miacid (MY-a-sid). This early meat-eater lived up to 60 million years ago in the vast forests that covered the earth at that time. Two types of miacid were significant in the

Meerkats and the mongoose family to which they belong are meat-eaters, or carnivores, and are part of the group of animals known as Viverridae. This family has thirty-six different subgroups called genera and within these there are seventy-one species.

ORDER

Carnivora
(carnivores)

SUPERFAMILY

Feloidea
(catlike forms)

FAMILY

Viverridae

SUBFAMILY

Herpestinae
African and Asian
mongooses

SUBFAMILY

Galidiinae
Madagascan
mongooses

MEERKAT GENUS

Suricata

SPECIES

suricatta

history of the Viverridae: the Vulpavines, found mainly in the Americas and similar in appearance to modern stoats, and the Viverravines that resembled the civets and genets of today's Viverridae family. In fact, these modern mammals retain many of the features of those early carnivores. They still live in trees and have a catlike nocturnal lifestyle. However, they have made advances in certain areas, such as having a well-developed inner ear.

The mongoose, although still retaining teeth structures from those early days, has made greater changes. As the climate altered, the forest began to give way to areas of drier grasslands and sandy open plains. Here small mammals bred in abundance and many carnivores, including mongooses, adjusted to a life in the open where there was plenty of food. Mongooses became predominantly insect-eaters,

---

MEERKATS HAVE EXCELLENT SIGHT AND CAN SPOT A BIRD OF PREY AT A GREAT DISTANCE

---

although some species included fruit in their diets and most ate small rodents and reptiles.

They left the trees to make their homes in burrows or rock crevices. As a result, their bodies changed to adapt to life on the ground. Some, like the savanna mongoose, lost the fifth digit on their paws that had helped them to climb, and their hind feet became longer so they could cover greater distances on the ground. Others, like the meerkat, developed long claws so they could dig out insects from under the soil and make their own burrows.

K. Ammann/Planet Earth Pictures

Ronald S. Rogoff/Planet Earth Pictures

The slender mongoose (above) *prefers a forest habitat and has short curved claws to help it to climb trees easily. It also lives in open country.*

Dwarf mongooses are highly sociable and active by day. At night they often shelter in termite mounds.

Ronald S. Rogoff/Planet Earth Pictures

Yellow mongooses (above) *live in groups of up to fifty animals. They prefer open country.*

There are many variations between different species of mongooses, and their shape and color depend on what they eat and where they live. Mongooses' coloring reflects their habitat—those, like the meerkat, that live in dry sandy areas are light in color, often gray or buff. They also have markings, such as dark tips to the tails or bands of

---

THE MARSH MONGOOSE IS THE
ONLY SPECIES TO POSSESS A
KEEN SENSE OF TOUCH

---

darker color across their backs, which help them blend in with their surroundings. But even within a single species there can be variation. The slender mongoose is generally gray or light brown; in the Kalahari Desert, however, it has red fur to blend in with the soil color. The small Indian mongoose is light gray in arid regions but is red speckled with black in wet tropical regions.

Broadly, mongooses can be divided into two groups: those that live on their own or with a mate and those that live in packs.

Solitary animals are usually nocturnal, coming out at night because they are less likely to be seen by their enemies. Not all solitary mongooses are nocturnal. The slender mongoose takes advantage of tree cover to hunt during the day, hiding from predators in the undergrowth. It is the most arboreal (tree-living) of all the mongooses and can shin up and down tree trunks like a squirrel.

Apart from the white-tailed mongoose—a handsome gray animal with dark legs and a white

1331

THE MONGOOSES' FAMILY TREE

tail—all the other mongooses found outside Africa belong to the genus *Herpestes*. They are solitary species, with the exception of the Egyptian mongoose, which sometimes lives alone and sometimes in a pack. Some Herpestes mongooses are nocturnal and others are active during the day.

The marsh mongoose, which lives south of the Sahara beside water, is dark with coarse fur and a short tapering tail. It is at home in water or on land and resembles an otter, except that it has no webbing between its toes.

The black-legged mongooses that live in east and west Africa are gray with long tails and black legs and have short sleek fur, giving them a tidier appearance than other mongooses.

SOCIAL MONGOOSES

Social mongooses, such as the meerkat, the banded mongoose, and the yellow mongoose, live on the open grassy plains or in the desert. They are diurnal (active during the day) and live in packs, which enable them to give each other warning of predators. They have a complex social system so that they can survive the dangers of life in the open.

Dwarf and banded mongooses prefer more tree cover than meerkats but they live in similar organized packs. The Angolan and Alexander's mongooses, as well as the Kusimanse, are social mongooses that live in west and central Africa.

Illustrations Simon Turvey/Wildlife Art Agency

HEADS AND TAILS

The shape of mongooses' heads varies according to their eating habits. Those, like the meerkat, that dart and snap at their prey to kill it, have longer snouts with sharper canine teeth than species such as the banded mongoose that catch less active prey. The fur on the head is much paler colored than on the rest of the body. The slender shape of the head also aids the burrowing habits of some species.

Although mongooses do not have perineal scent sacs like genets and civets, which are sought after by perfume manufacturers, they do have special anal glands, situated, either side of the long tail, which is a yellowish color with a black tip. They use these glands to mark territory and they produce a scent that lasts up to two weeks. When the secretions of the small Indian mongoose were analyzed they were found to contain six different acids, each with a unique smell. Individual mongooses have a different mixture, giving them a unique odor that is recognized by others of the same species.

The Indian gray mongoose has a gland underneath the whiskers on its face that gives off a honeylike smell that lasts for two days. Dwarf and banded mongooses rub their cheeks in a similar way to produce a scent.

There are twenty-seven species of African and Asian mongooses in thirteen genera and four species in four genera of Madagascan mongooses. The African and Asian mongooses are different from other Viverridae in that they do not have a pocket in each ear, called a bursa, although the yellow mongoose, which has very large ears, has a faint depression in the ear that could be the remains of a pocket. Some are solitary and others live in packs.

GENET

FOSSA

PALM CIVET

BANDED/ PALM CIVET

VIVERRIDAE

MEERKAT

Suricata suricatta
(*soor-ee-KA-ta soor-ee-KA-ta*)

Also known as the suricate, the meerkat lives in dens or burrows on the open plains of southern Africa around the Kalahari Desert. Altogether, twenty species of mongoose live in Africa. One, the Egyptian mongoose, has spread into Israel, Portugal, and southern Spain.

Mongooses that inhabit forests tend to follow a solitary lifestyle as they have plenty of cover from enemies. Those living in open country need the protection of a group.

OTHER AFRICAN SPECIES:
MARSH MONGOOSE   DWARF MONGOOSE
YELLOW MONGOOSE   KUSIMANSE

MADAGASCAR MONGOOSES

subfamily Galidiinae
(*gal-ID-in-a*)

There are four species in four genera. These mongooses are restricted to the island of Madagascar. When the island was separated from the rest of the African continent they were trapped in a limited habitat and began to develop differently from their counterparts on the mainland. They have a bursa, or ear flap, like other Viverridae families, and some, like the ring-tailed mongoose, have perineal scent glands. They are darker in color than some African and Asian species, are solitary, and prefer a higher density of tree cover. Many have rings or bands on their backs and tails.

SPECIES:
RING-TAILED MONGOOSE
BROAD-STRIPED MONGOOSE
NARROW-STRIPED MONGOOSE
BROWN MONGOOSE

INDIAN GRAY MONGOOSE

Herpestes edwardsi
(*her-PEST-ees ed-WARD-zi*)

The Indian gray mongoose is one of seven species living in Asia. It is found all over India, Sri Lanka, and in east and central Arabia to Nepal. It is a solitary mongoose that comes out by day and was the hero Rikki Tikki Tavi of Rudyard Kipling's tale from The Jungle Books about a dramatic fight between a mongoose and a snake. In parts of Malaysia this mongoose is kept as a pet and used to kill snakes. It has unwisely been introduced to other parts of the world to rid areas of unwanted rodents, but while ridding the areas of rodents, it has also been destructive to native birds.

FALANOUC

FANALOKA

ANATOMY:
THE MEERKAT

HEAD SHAPE

The long and tapering head helps the meerkat.

The ears of the meerkat are adapted to its digging lifestyle. Each ear has a series of ridges and flaps. By bringing the top ridge down and the back ridge forward, it is able to close them up.

The meerkat (above, center) has a body length of 12 in (30 cm) and a tail length of 7 in (18 cm). The largest mongoose is the white-tailed mongoose, with a body length of 23 in (58 cm) and a tail of 17 in (43 cm). The tiny dwarf mongoose has a combined body and tail length of 17 in (43 cm).

FACE MARKINGS

Color in mongooses is for camouflage so that they are hidden from both their prey and their predators. The dark rings around the eyes make the eyes look much larger than they really are. This is important in hunting and defense for it tricks the prey or predator into believing it is confronting an animal larger than it really is.

BODY SHAPE

A low-slung body with short legs is a feature of mongooses, making it easy for them to pursue prey underground. The long body of the meerkat enables it to sit up and look around for predators.

X RAY

The structure of the meerkat's skeleton is slim and rangy. It has a long flexible neck, backbone, and tail. The tail is used for balancing or signaling. Feet and legs are adapted to walking on two or four legs.

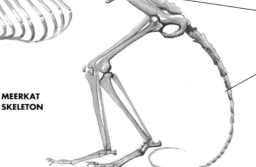

MEERKAT SKELETON

long strong sp

long tail used fo balance

HANDS AND FEET

The meerkat uses its hands, or forepaws, for eating and for activities like grooming its fellow pack members. They are also useful for cuffing a disobedient infant. The marsh mongoose has very sensitive hands with a highly developed sense of touch. It picks up stones with its hands as it searches for crabs and insects.

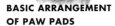

digital pads

planter pads

metacarpal/ metatarsal pads

BASIC ARRANGEMENT OF PAW PADS

Forepaw

Hind foot

CLASSIFICATION

GENUS: *SURICATA*

SPECIES: *SURICATTA*

SIZE

HEAD–BODY LENGTH/MALE: 12–13 IN (30–33 CM)

SHOULDER HEIGHT/MALE: 6 IN (15 CM)

TAIL LENGTH/MALE: 7–9 IN (18–23 CM)

WEIGHT/MALE: 22–34 OZ (623–964 G)

WEIGHT AT BIRTH: 1.16 OZ (33 G) [IN TWYCROSS ZOO, ENGLAND]

COLORATION

GROUND COLOR: GRAY COAT WITH REDDISH TINGE AND PALER UNDERPARTS

DARKER STRIPES ACROSS LOWER BACK AND TAIL

BLACK TIP TO TAIL

FEATURES

DARK PATCHES AROUND EYES

LONG CLAWS FOR DIGGING

UPRIGHT STANCE WHEN ON THE ALERT

NARROW BODY FOR BURROWING

LONG TAIL

The meerkat's long tail acts as a balance.

FEET AND CLAWS

The meerkat has claws 0.5 in (13 mm) long for digging. Hind feet are often elongated and adapted to life on the ground. Unlike other mongooses, meerkats have only four toes on their feet.

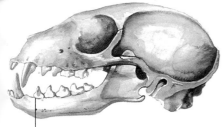

SKULL OF MEERKAT (side view)

interlocking cusped teeth

This meerkat's skull shape is typical of the insect-eating mongooses.

The yellow mongoose is mainly a meat-eater, or carnivore. Because of this it has sharp canine teeth for tearing meat.

long canine teeth

SKULL OF YELLOW MONGOOSE (side view)

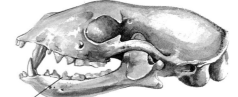

blunt molars

SKULL OF BLACK-LEGGED MONGOOSE (side view)

Because it is an omnivore, the teeth of the black-legged mongoose are blunt to cope with a variety of foods.

BURROWERS AND DIGGERS

FROM SPECIES THAT LIVE A LIFE ALONE TO OTHERS WITH HIGHLY ORGANIZED FAMILIES OF MIDWIVES, TEACHERS, AND SENTRIES ·

The mongoose family is successful and widespread. The ancient Egyptians considered the mongoose a sacred animal, and wall paintings depicting these little carnivores, dating back to 2800 B.C., have been found in temples and tombs.

While the solitary species of mongoose generally show aggression to others of the same species, social mongooses, like the meerkat, live in friendly colonies. They have a pack territory that they will defend against an intruding group, but there is little aggression between pack members.

These pack mongooses emerge from their dens in the morning, popping their heads out of their burrows to sniff the air before coming out to sit slumped in the sunshine, to groom themselves and one another, and perhaps to mate. Then they set

SENSES

Most mongooses have a very well-developed sense of smell, especially those that live in burrows and have to seek prey from under the ground. The Egyptian mongoose earned its Greek name *ichneumon*, or "tracker," because of its ability to sniff out prey; it seems to have a more acute sense of smell than any other mongoose.

Although the Egyptian mongoose has only average vision it appears to have some sensitivity to color, like the meerkat and the Indian gray mongoose. Only the meerkat, the banded mongoose, and the dwarf mongoose have excellent sight, which is very necessary in their exposed habitat. Other diurnal mongooses have limited vision but the sense of hearing is acute in all species.

off for several hours of foraging, either returning to the den or resting in the shade in the midday heat. They return to the burrow in the evening, where they resume their social activities for a short time before dusk when they retire for the night.

Dwarf mongooses in Kenya have developed an unusual partnership with insect-eating birds, in particular two species of bush hornbill. They forage together, the hornbills sharing the insects that the mongooses discover. In turn, the birds utter warning cries when predators appear—even when these pose no danger to themselves. If the mongooses are not about when the hornbills arrive for the daily expedition, the birds will wait outside the burrows,

> MONGOOSES APPEAR TO ENJOY
> PLAYING; MOST OF THEIR PLAY
> ACTIVITY IN THE WILD IS RELATED
> TO AGGRESSION

sometimes even putting their beaks down the holes and calling! Hornbills eat rodents but they do not eat baby dwarf mongooses.

Although the social mongooses appear friendly natured, there is little interaction between species. The meerkat and yellow mongoose occasionally inhabit the same burrow and the meerkat sometimes lives alongside the ground squirrel, taking advantage of its burrow. Dwarf and banded mongooses may be found in the same territory, but there is no competition for dens as the dwarf species can squeeze into much smaller holes than its larger relatives.

In the heat of the day, meerkats love to rest together in the shade. This is the time for grooming each other and watching the youngsters at play .

David Macdonald/Oxford Scientific Films

HABITAT

Mongooses favor three climatic regions in particular, although they will overlap from one to another, and some are able to survive in drier conditions than others. The tropical rain forest, where the climate is hot and humid with little variation in temperature, is home to a number of solitary mongoose species.

The ring-tailed mongoose lives in the forests of Madagascar where it digs a burrow or lives in holes in trees. It is a good climber and can also swim, but has to stay near tree cover because it cannot cope with hot sun. The slender mongoose, although it also lives happily in more open areas, is a good tree climber and will make its home in forests.

Farther away from the equator, where tropical or moist savanna or grassland occurs, mongooses will also be found. Here there is a dry and a rainy season, although temperatures remain high. The ground is covered with tall grass and scattered trees, which provide cover for different animals, and in the rainy season there is an abundance of food. Lakes and rivers that run through the grasslands have trees along their banks and are home to species like the marsh mongoose. It lives in any watery area, including papyrus and mangrove swamps, and feeds on aquatic insects and animals.

Dwarf and banded mongooses favor the savanna, preferring areas where there are trees rather than simply open grassland, and they will use termite mounds for their dens, as well as holes in the ground, rock crevices, and hollow trees.

Meerkat on sentry duty. Sentries often climb to the top of a tree stump, rock, or other elevated site in order to get a better view of their surroundings.

Clem Haagner/Ardea

The meerkat can exist in more open and drier habitats than most other mongooses. It is found in near-desert conditions, particularly in the Kalahari Desert of southern Africa. It does not need to drink regularly, finding what moisture it needs in the roots and tubers of plants or by chewing tsama melons. It likes to make its den in ground that is harder than sand, particularly favoring the banks of dry riverbeds and fossil lakes.

TERRITORIES AND DENS

Solitary mongooses tend to be agressive to members of their own species; males are highly territorial and guard against intruding males, although younger nonbreeding males are sometimes tolerated. Their territories overlap with the territories of

DISTRIBUTION

Mongooses are widespread and are found in Europe and Asia as well as Africa and Madagascar.

In the 19th century they were introduced to the Hawaiian Islands and West Indies to kill rats and snakes but they ended up raiding farms and eating poultry, as well as causing havoc with native wildlife. As mongooses are considered potentially injurious to other wildlife and poultry, some countries, including the United States, allow importation only for scientific and educational purposes.

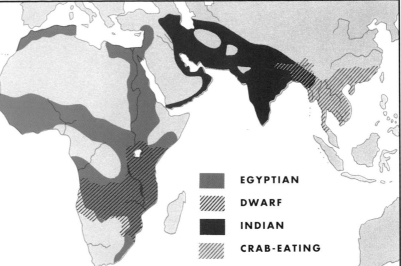

EGYPTIAN

DWARF

INDIAN

CRAB-EATING

Because of their highly developed sense of smell, meerkats are able to locate underground grubs.

one or more females. They may have a series of paths—sometimes even recognized footpaths—which they scamper along regularly, and if they meet another male they will threaten or even attack it. Females have smaller territories and tend to remain within them, breeding and rearing young in a den or burrow.

Pack mongooses that inhabit more open plains have territories related to the amount of food available. In the Serengeti, where the savanna is drier than elsewhere and food supplies scarcer, banded mongooses may have a home range of 5.8 sq miles (15 sq km) and travel over 5.6 miles (9 km) in a day. But in Ruwenzori Park in Uganda, they have a range of only 0.4 sq miles (1 sq km) and travel less than 1.2 miles (2 km) per day. Meerkats have a home territory of 4 sq miles (10 sq km) or more and they forage over a different section each day,

EARS THAT CLOSE UP FOR BURROWING

Meerkats and yellow mongooses are especially good at digging. To protect their ears from flying soil that might get inside and block them or cause infection, these mongooses have developed a special device that enables them to close up their ears when needed. Each ear has a series of ridges and flaps. By bringing the top ridge down and the back ridge forward the mongoose is able to close up the opening in the ear, keeping any airborne earth out.

Clem Haagner/Ardea

returning to the first area after a week when the food supply has had time to replenish itself.

Within their territory, mongooses live in holes in trees, rocks, or in burrows. Meerkats have a den that consists of half a dozen warrens 165–330 ft (50–100 m) apart, each occupied for a few months at a time. Their burrows are a complex series of tunnels interspersed with small chambers 1 ft (30 cm) high and 6 in (15 cm) long. The burrows may have as many as fifteen entrances and cover an

---

LIKE OTHER DESERT DWELLERS, MEERKATS HAVE EVOLVED WAYS OF COPING WITH TEMPERATURE EXTREMES

---

area some 16 ft (4.8 m) across. Throughout their range they have a number of bolt holes which offer cover in the more exposed areas. They dig these themselves, but, although they are excellent diggers, they prefer to occupy burrows made by other animals, such as the ground squirrel, with whom they live in partnership.

Meerkats, like other animals that live in the desert extremes of temperature, have evolved a way of coping with the heat. Their dens are built at

FOCUS ON

KALAHARI DESERT

Desert is defined as a place where less than 10 in (25 cm) of rain falls in a year. Yet in the Kalahari, which covers 200,770 sq miles (520,000 sq km) of southwest Africa, some years may bring more than twice that amount, and others barely any. The rain that doesn't evaporate in the heat is quickly soaked up by the hot ground, and grass and vegetation spring up in abundance. This attracts herds of grazing animals that, in turn, bring insects and predators onto the plains. The Kalahari has three seasons. Rains begin any time from November to January and last till March or even May. This is followed by a cold dry season from June to August and a hot dry season from September until the rain comes, usually in November or December.

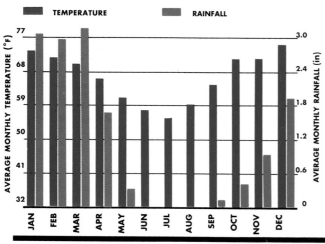

TEMPERATURE AND RAINFALL

■ TEMPERATURE   ■ RAINFALL

Chart: Average monthly temperature (°F), y-axis values 32, 41, 50, 59, 68, 77. Average monthly rainfall (in), y-axis values 0, 0.6, 1.2, 1.8, 2.4, 3.0. Months along x-axis: JAN, FEB, MAR, APR, MAY, JUN, JUL, AUG, SEP, OCT, NOV, DEC.

Described as a desert, the Kalahari is a thirstland, or semidesert. It is dry for much of the year, during which time the plants become bleached by the sun. When the rains do arrive, the plants recover with great speed. Dry salt pans are a feature of the Kalahari. These areas are the flattest of all landforms.

several levels, some 6.5 ft (2 m) below ground. While the temperature outside in the burning sun may fluctuate during the day, the deepest tunnels only change by 33.8°F (1°C), even in summer. Those nearer the surface may change by 73.4°F (23°C) in summer and 50°F (10°C) in winter, but compared with summer fluctuations above ground of 109.4°F (43°C) and winter ones of 64.4°F (18°C), this is a considerable improvement. In cold weather, meerkats tend to remain longer in their dens, while in hot weather they rest in the shade. ■

NEIGHBORS

The Kalahari supports a rich diversity of wildlife. Many of its animals are permanent residents but others pass through after the rains to feed on the lush vegetation.

HONEY BADGER

The honey badger, or ratel, is a ferocious hunter that, like the meerkat, will attack venomous snakes.

SPRINGBOK

Springboks are elegant gazelles. They live in herds and and are known for their spectacular leaps into the air.

Illustrations Edwina Goldstone

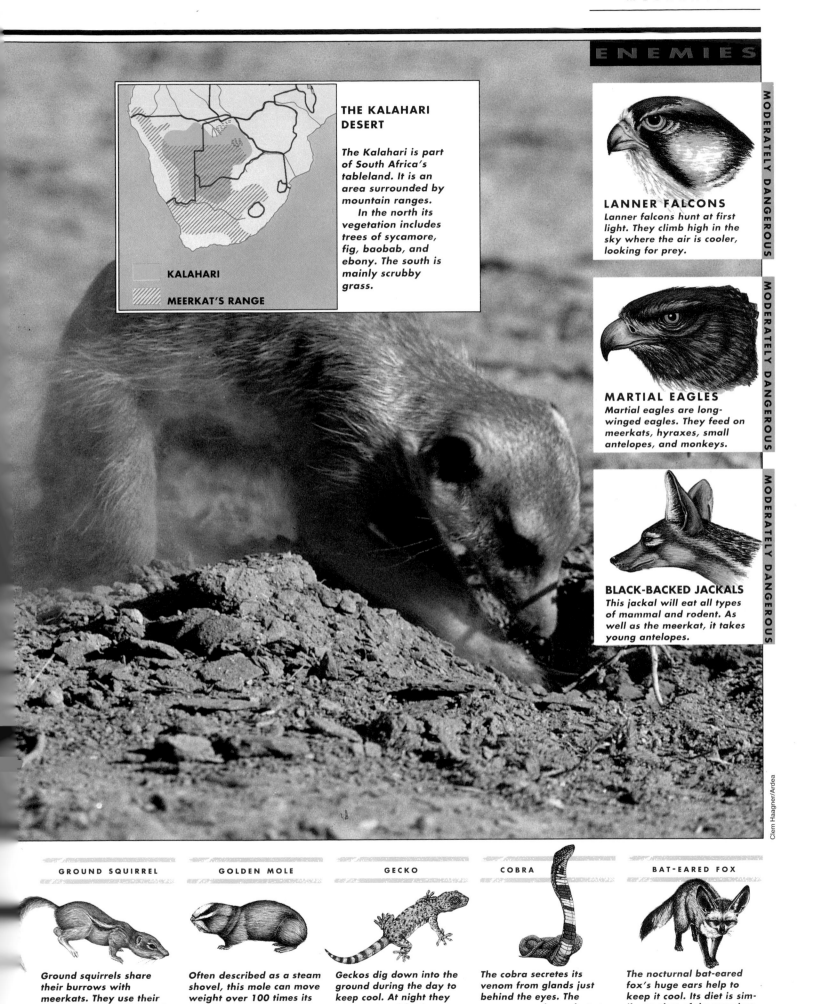

ENEMIES

THE KALAHARI DESERT

The Kalahari is part of South Africa's tableland. It is an area surrounded by mountain ranges.

In the north its vegetation includes trees of sycamore, fig, baobab, and ebony. The south is mainly scrubby grass.

☐ KALAHARI

▨ MEERKAT'S RANGE

LANNER FALCONS
Lanner falcons hunt at first light. They climb high in the sky where the air is cooler, looking for prey.

MARTIAL EAGLES
Martial eagles are long-winged eagles. They feed on meerkats, hyraxes, small antelopes, and monkeys.

BLACK-BACKED JACKALS
This jackal will eat all types of mammal and rodent. As well as the meerkat, it takes young antelopes.

MODERATELY DANGEROUS

MODERATELY DANGEROUS

MODERATELY DANGEROUS

Clem Haagner/Ardea

GROUND SQUIRREL

Ground squirrels share their burrows with meerkats. They use their tails as parasols during the very hot weather.

GOLDEN MOLE

Often described as a steam shovel, this mole can move weight over 100 times its own but cannot reverse against the lie of its fur.

GECKO

Geckos dig down into the ground during the day to keep cool. At night they come out and feed on scorpions and insects.

COBRA

The cobra secretes its venom from glands just behind the eyes. The venom runs down ducts to reach the snake's fangs.

BAT-EARED FOX

The nocturnal bat-eared fox's huge ears help to keep it cool. Its diet is similar to that of the meerkat and includes scorpions.

FOOD AND FEEDING

Mongooses are classified as carnivores; although they do eat small mammals, many of them, like the meerkat, have a diet that consists largely of insects. Some species also eat fruits and vegetables.

After a time of relaxation in front of their burrows, meerkats set out each day to search for food. Most of their insect prey shelters under rocks or in burrows and they zigzag from side to side, pushing their noses under stones and into rotting tree trunks or digging furiously into the soil. As they forage they keep up a shambling run.

Although meerkats forage as a group, each one hunts for its own food rather than working as part of a team. Nevertheless, if a meerkat scents a gecko under the ground, another may join in to help and will share in the prize at the end. Because they are noisy foragers, a dwarf mongoose that discovers an ants' nest will let out such excited squeaks that it will inevitably draw others to share in the feast.

FEEDING TECHNIQUES

Ways of eating vary between different species of mongoose. The meerkat eats mice or lizards by holding the creature in its claws and tearing at it with its teeth, whereas the slender mongoose eats small animals from the head down, leaving only the feet, tail, and skin. Some species give a "death shake" to kill their prey.

Some mongooses will break open their prey on

MEERKAT AND SCORPION

When the meerkat comes face-to-face with a scorpion it uses its agility and speed to avoid the poison in the tail, which is strong enough to kill a child. Then it strikes

out with a front paw. The meerkat attempts to bite the tail off at the beginning of an attack thereby rendering the scorpion harmless before finishing its meal.

Illustrations John Cox/Wildlife Art Agency

PREY

Mongooses eat insects, small mammals, reptiles, and some fruits. Among their victims are poisonous snakes and scorpions. The mongooses build up an immunity to the venom.

MILLIPEDE

Illustrations John Cox/Wildlife Art Agency

FIRST MOVES

When mongoose and cobra confront each other the mongoose attacks the head of the snake.

WRESTLING MATCH

Each bout of fighting lasts only a few seconds. During the fight the animals roll over each other, either one being on the top.

VICTORY

The mongoose must be careful to stay out of striking distance of the cobra. Only when the snake tires sufficiently and drops its head after a strike, can the mongoose leap in for the kill.

rocks. They do this by taking a snail, an egg, or a shell, and throwing it backward between their hind legs against a hard surface until it cracks open. The marsh mongoose eats a diet of fish and other aquatic animals. It has tough back molars to help it crack open the hard shells of some prey.

Most mongooses need to drink. Some, like the ring-tailed mongoose from Madagascar, need a supply of water. The meerkat can survive without water and will eat fruit when it is very thirsty. ■

KILLING TACTICS

The Egyptian mongoose has a clever tactic for catching mammals and birds. Like a weasel, it first attracts their attention by performing extraordinary antics—chasing its tail and leaping up and down. Curiosity brings the victim within the Egyptian mongoose's range. In a flash, it lunges, catching the animal in its jaws and killing it with a sharp bite on the neck.

As well as insects, the Egyptian mongoose is partial to reptiles, small mammals, and birds and will even eat fish.

Illustrations John Cox

MOUSE	LIZARD	SNAIL	FINCH	DUNG BEETLE	SCORPION

SOCIAL STRUCTURE

Despite their name, even solitary mongooses may live in packs of up to six or so, comprising a male, one or two females, and their young. The male's territory is often large and may overlap with those of several females with whom it will mate. Truly social species, like the meerkat and dwarf and banded mongooses, have a highly organized society with a remarkable degree of cooperation between members.

By living in a pack, mongooses can keep a lookout for predators and warn each other of their approach, take care of each other in danger or distress, look after the young, and band together to attack an enemy.

The meerkat lives in groups of up to thirty and may integrate a lone outsider into the group without hostility. Males and females often leave the pack to join another or, occasionally, to start up their own. The home range of the meerkat may cover 4 sq miles (10 sq km) or more. Territories are marked with scent, especially the bushes and rocks closest to the dens, which are the center of activity.

The yellow mongoose (right) is a sociable mongoose and often lives in much larger groups than meerkats. Litters are usually of one to four young.

Carol Hughes/Bruce Coleman Ltd.

in SIGHT

MEERKAT'S VISION

Meerkats have very acute daylight vision and can spot a bird of prey in the sky when it is a speck on the horizon. Because the pupil of its eye is very long from side to side it has a wide field of vision enabling it to see over a greater distance without moving its head. It has a special membrane that pulls down over the eye to protect it when digging.

The pack has a system of responsibilities. Usually the males undertake "sentry duty," taking turns keeping watch for an hour or so while the others forage. They will generally climb up to a vantage point, such as a tree or a tall rock, to get a better view of how the land lies. When they spot a predator they give out loud warning cries and the other meerkats immediately stand motionless on their hind legs with their paws hanging down. If necessary, they will dart down the nearest bolt hole, which they make in the

ALERT MIDWIFE

A midwife watches over a group of youngsters. All the time they are in her care she will be on guard and may remain so for hours. The main sentry picks the highest vantage point in the area.

Illustrations Peter David Scott/Wildlife Art Agency

SCENT MARKING

The anal pouches of meerkats contain strong-smelling scent. Males frequently scent mark around the den entrance on both vertical and horizontal surfaces. Before doing so, they will sniff around the area. After emptying the gland, they often rub their bodies on the marked area. Scent marking is also done with urine when males cock their rear legs like dogs up vertical surfaces. Communal latrines are used by each group.

GROUP GUARDS

While a circle of meerkat sentries protects the young, a juvenile checks out the burrow of a ground squirrel.

course of foraging, digging together as a team.

A nursing meerkat mother needs to forage in order to keep up her milk supply, so baby-sitters take turns staying in the den to look after her babies. As many as five, males as well as females, may stay behind and they will also care for young from other packs that wander into the territory.

Pack mongooses will go to great lengths to aid another in distress. Dwarf mongooses, which have a dominant, or alpha, male and female pair, have been known to make great efforts to rescue an injured animal. The alpha male will attempt to dig out pack members trapped in caved-in tunnels and may mount an attack on a predator that has caught a victim. Meerkats will also aid a wounded or sick creature. In one instance, a nursing female that was attacked and injured by a bird of prey was escorted to her den by the pack. She was fed and her babies cared for until she recovered.

DEFENSE AND ATTACK

Meerkats are sometimes aggressive toward other groups of meerkats. Smaller packs will give way to larger ones, although equally matched groups will sometimes attack each other, rushing forward with tails bristling, lunging and scrabbling in a noisy battle. Solitary species, like the slender

David Keith Jones

A group of banded mongooses (left) *on a termite mound.*

mongoose, will attack a threatening male by biting at its head and shoulders.

Mongooses have several methods of defense and attack that may be observed as they play. By bristling their fur they can make themselves seem bigger than they are. They will snap at danger and dart their heads backward and forward with open mouths to indicate aggression. Some species will turn away from a rival and bite at it over their shoulders or between their hind legs, or roll over onto their backs to use their teeth and claws.

Larger mongooses will often frighten off enemies by moving forward in a close-knit group. The banded mongoose will form a cluster when alarmed, with the youngest and most vulnerable in

GROUP DEFENSE

The banded mongoose is particularly adept at intimidating predators. When an enemy is sighted, these mongooses rush together to form a tight group and begin to move forward in a mob, swaying from side to side. Sometimes one or two individuals will rise to their hind legs giving the impression of a large animal moving purposefully forward. This is accompanied by a combination of growls and snaps and is enough to deter an enemy as daunting as a jackal. In fact, these intrepid mongooses will go so far as to chase even a large predator and snap at its heels or tail.

Banded mongooses will even rescue a group member from the clutches of a predator, harrying the enemy until it lets go.

ENEMY SPOTTED

A band of vigilant meerkats come across a startled bat-eared fox at its den.

UNITED

Tails erect and fur bristling, the meerkats advance as one.

TAKE OFF

The fox turns tail and the meerkats give chase. The danger has passed and peace is restored.

the center. Meerkats rush to protect their young, covering them with their bodies.

Numbers of breeding males and females in a pack of meerkats will live peacefully together. When danger threatens, the largest and strongest male will take a lead in defense but he does not attempt to dominate the pack. Dwarf mongooses have a more pronounced hierarchy, the oldest male and female being the dominant breeding pair. The alpha male takes the initiative in the care of the pack, rescuing pack members caught by predators, while the female usually leads foraging parties.

VOCALIZATION

Social mongooses use a great many sounds to communicate with each other. When they are playing they make gentle peeping sounds, rising to a louder twitter when excited. Whistles or loud barks indicate alarm.

Sound is important to social mongooses; while they are concentrating on looking for food they cannot see if they have become cut off from the group or if there is danger close by. When they set off to forage they have a special "moving out" call. Thereafter different sounds indicate that they have found something exciting, or that there is a predator in the immediate vicinity.

Meerkat females make more noise than males, keeping up a soft murmuring. A cross clucking sound is used to scold a disobedient youngster. Babies "cheep" continually and purr when content.

SOCIAL GROOMING

The time a meerkat spends relaxing before setting out to forage each morning is important to the whole group relationship. This is when it grooms the fur of its fellows—a useful activity that helps to maintain the amicable relationship these animals have with one another. ∎

Illustration John Morris/Wildlife Art Agency

LIFE CYCLE

For their size, mongooses are slow to mature and reproduce. They live for about ten years and breed from the age of two. This applies to the dwarf mongoose as well, whose smaller size might suggest a shorter life span.

COURTSHIP

When the female is ready to mate, she sometimes engages in mock fights with the male, jumping and snapping at him. The dwarf and Egyptian mongooses are much more gentle, mutually grooming each other and making soft noises as a prelude to mating. In most species the female will crouch and then run away, with her tail in the air, encouraging the male to follow her. This may occur a number of times before she allows the male to mate.

BIRTH

Some species, such as the dwarf mongoose and the meerkat, have several litters a year. Their deliveries coincide with the rainy season, when there is plenty of food. There are more litters born in areas where there is an abundant supply of food. Banded mongooses that are living in a warm climate where there is plenty to eat may have four litters in a year, but the same species in a less productive area will only breed in the rainy season. Egyptian mongooses only have one litter a year, but may have a second if their first brood is lost.

A litter can consist of between one and six young, but most commonly there are three or four babies, born after a gestation of sixty days. Gestation does vary, though, between thirty-five days in the dwarf mongoose and eighty days in the slender mongoose. Most young are hardly able to move when they are born and they are blind and deaf with very little fur. Their adult markings are

COURTSHIP

When the female is ready to mate she jumps up and down in front of the male in mock battle.

PLAY LEARNING

When they leave the den at about five weeks of age, the day is spent playing and learning how to defend themselves. By the time they are two they will be ready to mate.

in SIGHT

ALPHA MALES AND FEMALES

Dwarf mongooses have a breeding hierarchy not found among meerkats. The oldest male and female are the only breeding pair, and all other members of the pack help to feed and look after their babies. The "alpha" female usually remains dominant for several years, and then another female takes over.

Other females do mate within the pack, but they tend to abort or lose their young. This may be because the alpha female kills all infants so that their mothers can suckle her babies. The dominant female will allow the other males to mate with her only after the alpha male has lost interest.

Clem Haagner/Ardea

GROWING UP
The life of a young meerkat

Illustrations Mike Donnolly/Wildlife Art Agency

OUTSIDE THE DEN

One to four young are born in a nursery den. At about five weeks of age they take their first look at the world outside.

WEANING

The young will continue to suckle from the mother until they are about nine weeks of age.

THE NEXT LITTER

The mother will be ready to mate again the following year in September or October. Her next litter will be born in November or December.

babies are then transported by the mother or a baby-sitter, who carries each one by the nape of the neck. Baby dwarf mongooses are sometimes brought outside when they are only a day old, and the baby-sitter will groom and lick them in the sunshine.

When the babies are two to four weeks old their eyes open, and they leave the nest soon afterward. They begin to eat food other than milk at about the age of three weeks or even less, and are fully weaned by nine weeks, earlier in some species.

To maintain her supply of milk the mother must leave the den to find food. Other mongooses baby-sit while she is away, males as well as females, and as the babies grow these surrogate parents bring insects and other food for them to eat. They also play with the babies.

Adolescent young have a difficult role to play. While still at the stage of begging for food from the adults for themselves they are obliged to pass it on to the new babies, doing so with obvious reluctance. As the young develop, the mother teaches them to forage by holding prey in her mouth and encouraging them to chase her and snap at it while she runs about.

As they grow older and emerge from the den each baby meerkat is assigned a "tutor" who has the responsibility of teaching it to hunt. This mongoose, usually an adult male, will bring the young live prey to deal with, and the babies fight to keep other young away from "their" teacher. In this way they learn to deal with such prey as scorpions and ants, both of which are dangerous or painful if handled wrongly. It is some time before they learn to tackle large prey such as the cobra, and occasionally they end up the loser. ■

barely recognizable. The narrow-striped mongoose, however, is an exception to this rule, as the young have visible stripes at birth and their eyes are open.

The babies are born in a nest in the mother's den, which may be hidden away in a rock crevice, a termite mound, or a hollow tree. Mongooses feed their newborn infants in a sitting position, curled forward. As the babies grow, the female will lie on her back or her side to suckle. To get rid of waste the mother stimulates the babies to defecate by licking them and consuming their feces. Mongooses frequently move from one den to another and the

FRIEND OR FOE?

MANY SPECIES OF MONGOOSE ARE NUMEROUS AND EVEN REGARDED AS PESTS. THOSE THAT LIVE IN RAIN FORESTS, HOWEVER, ARE HAVING THEIR HOMES RAPIDLY DESTROYED—AND THEIR LIVES

Mongooses are hardy animals. They can often adapt to changes in habitat and diet, and some species will even live in close proximity to people. In certain parts of the world they are so prolific that they are regarded as pests. In others they are at risk from the destruction of their habitat and none more so than the rare Liberian and bushy-tailed mongooses whose rain-forest homes are fast disappearing.

Each year, thousands of square miles of the earth's rain forest is bulldozed and burned. In west Africa only a fraction of the vast forest that covered Liberia, Ghana, the Ivory Coast, and Sierra Leone

remains, as loggers and farmers have systematically felled the trees. The Liberian mongoose, whose habitat is restricted to this small area of Africa, is in danger of extinction. In India the rate of deforestation has also been rapid and very little natural habitat is left. Half of the land is cultivated for rice. This and other agriculture and urbanization have altered the landscape completely. In other Asian countries the pattern is the same and soon forest-dwelling mongooses will have nowhere to go.

The destruction of the rain forest has an effect on climate, reducing the amount of rainfall and increasing annual temperatures. Annual rainfall

MADAGASCAR

Madagascar is separated from Africa by the Mozambique channel. It has a range of climates and supports many unique birds and animals. The high land in the center is mixed evergreen and deciduous forest. To the south there are semiarid grasslands. The east coast was once carpeted with rich tropical rain forest. Only a fifth remains.

As early as 1927 it was recognized that the unique quality of wildlife on Madagascar needed some protection, and between 1927 and 1952 a dozen nature reserves were established followed by two national parks. Unlike national parks in other countries, these were not designed to attract tourists. They were set apart in the most isolated regions where it was hoped that a range of species would be protected from human interference and be allowed to continue undisturbed.

Nick Garbutt/Planet Earth Pictures

Konrad Wothe/Bruce Coleman Ltd.

The map shows the former and current areas of rain forest in Africa and Asia.

■ FORMER ■ CURRENT

It is estimated that each year 63,000 sq mi (160,000 sq km) of the earth's rain forest is either bulldozed for hardwood exports or burned for farming and urbanization.

In India the rate of deforestation is 510 sq mi (1,320 sq km) a week. The loss of the forest has affected the climate and reduced the annual rainfall south of Bombay by 157 in (399 cm).

south of Bombay has dropped from 390 in (991 cm) to 240 in (610 cm) This, in turn, contributes to a process known as desertification. An ever-increasing population in Africa cuts down trees and shrubs on the edge of the desert to provide fuel and building material and grazes its sheep and goats on the sparse vegetation. Crops are grown, too, and when the soil loses its fertility the people move on, leaving behind a wasteland where nothing can survive. This devastated area soon becomes part of the desert and in Mali the desert has spread over 220 miles (354 km) in only twenty years.

Elsewhere in Africa the scrub and scattered trees that provide the mongoose with shelter are cut down and replaced with uniform grasslands for grazing livestock. In Botswana, near the Kalahari

In Madagascar the local people use a technique known as slash and burn. Areas of forest are burned to grow crops. When the soil erodes, the land becomes useless and forest habitats are lost forever.

1351

Desert, there is extensive cattle ranching to supply the demands of the hamburger market in the West. In the face of this expanding area where prey and cover are scarce, animals are forced to retreat.

Certain species of mongoose are hunted for their meat. In the Kisangani area of Zaire, where there are few cattle, the kusimanse makes up 52 percent of all carnivore meat eaten by the Bakumu people. Although there is no immediate concern about these mongooses, the growth in human population threatens their habitat and increases the risk of overhunting.

BANDED MONGOOSES HAVE
ADAPTED TO LIVING IN DRY AREAS
FROM THEIR NORMAL HABITAT
OF FOREST MARGINS

Habitat destruction is a difficult process to halt. The needs of the poor are often pitted against the need for conservation. National parks have been introduced in many countries to preserve species under threat and 3 percent of India, 7 percent of Nepal, and 20 percent of Bhutan are set apart in this way. However, in India some of these reserves are bordered by hostile local people who want to use the land to provide themselves with the essentials for survival. In the Sokoke Reserve in Kenya, an important habitat for the bushy-tailed mongoose, sawed tree stumps and logs indicate that it is not always easy to maintain a protected area.

A meerkat chasing a snake in its Kalahari home, a habitat that is in no way endangered.

MONGOOSES IN DANGER

THE CHART BELOW SHOWS HOW THE INTERNATIONAL UNION FOR THE CONSERVATION OF NATURE (IUCN), OR THE WORLD CONSERVATION UNION, LISTS THE FOLLOWING SPECIES AS HAVING CONSERVATION CONCERN:

MADAGASCAR	BROAD-STRIPED MONGOOSE NARROW-STRIPED MONGOOSE BROWN MONGOOSE
AFRICA	ANGOLAN MONGOOSE LIBERIAN MONGOOSE POUSARGUES' MONGOOSE BUSHY-TAILED MONGOOSE
ASIA	SUMATRAN COLLARED MONGOOSE

NONE OF THE ABOVE HAS, AS YET, BEEN CLASSIFIED BY THE IUCN AS ENDANGERED. HOWEVER, ALL THE ABOVE SPECIES GIVE CAUSE FOR CONCERN.

David Macdonald/Oxford Scientific Films

The mongoose's success as a species is helped by its ability to adapt to a changing environment. Some, like the meerkat, live in semidesert areas, which are spreading. Some that live in forests are beginning to move out, such as the banded mongoose.

Although all species prefer some form of vegetation for cover, they can live on the margins of their preferred habitat and, like the urban fox in Britain, some species have even learned to live in close proximity to man.

Some animals, like the giant panda whose diet consists mainly of bamboo shoots, are specialist feeders. This is not true of the mongoose. Most species will eat anything from small mammals and reptiles to fruit, and many are particularly fond of insects. If the food it prefers is in short supply, the mongoose is adaptable and will eat whatever food is available. Those living by the sea will eat crabs and shellfish, while those living close to cultivated areas may take advantage of fields of corn or bananas. ∎

INTO THE FUTURE

For most mongoose species the future looks good. Indeed, in areas where they are thriving, local people regard them as pests. Even in Madagascar, where their status is of some concern due to the destruction of their habitat, mongooses may be legally killed if they are preying on poultry or feeding on crops. So prolific are they that in some parts of the world there are major schemes to eradicate them—and many of those end in failure.

Mongooses are valuable to scientists because they have changed little from their miacid ancestors. They therefore provide an evolutionary link between those early carnivores and the larger present-day species, such as the big cats, that have developed further. Studies of the mongoose will help us to understand how carnivores developed. In other ways, too, they are of interest to scientists. Their methods of communication by scent marking

PREDICTION

CAPTIVE BREEDING

It has been recommended by the IUCN that both the Liberian and bushy-tailed mongooses be introduced to zoos and bred in captivity to increase their numbers. The success of this rests with enough specimens being available for effective breeding programs.

may provide information on a little-understood process, and those that have a resistance to snake venom may help in the study of immunity.

It is important, therefore, to protect those species that are so scarce that they have been rarely seen by scientists, let alone studied, and their existence is only known through a few specimens and the descriptions of local people. There may be other species as yet undiscovered.

For those mongooses that have become isolated in small patches of rain forest there is increasing concern. Reserves and captive-breeding programs may not be able to save them. The Liberian mongoose is the most threatened of all species, followed closely by the bushy-tailed mongoose of central Africa. The habitat of both species is disappearing at an alarming rate, and they are now so rarely seen that it will be difficult, or impossible, to capture enough animals to start a captive-breeding program.

LIBERIAN MONGOOSE

Classed by the IUCN as the most vulnerable of all mongoose species, until a few years ago this shy creature was known only through a handful of skulls. Black, with two lighter stripes from ear to shoulder, it lives in groups of three to five and is active during the day. It lives on a specialized diet of beetle larvae and earthworms.

As it only inhabits places where there is deep sand, in the rapidly decreasing rain forests of west Africa it is fast disappearing. Not only is its habitat diminishing rapidly, but it is a favorite dish of local people. Now they, too, have reported that it is declining.

Kevin Schafter/NHPA

RABIES RISK

After its introduction to the West Indies, the Small Indian mongoose was found to be a carrier of rabies, and many of the endemic animals began to die of rabieslike symptoms. On Grenada, where rabies is rife, 0.4 percent of the country's annual income is set aside to destroy the rabies-carrying mongoose population, to no avail. Recently it was discovered that half the mongoose population is immune to the disease, and so by feeding the animals bait drenched in rabies vaccine, the government hopes that all mongooses will become immune.

Illustration Robin Budden/Wildlife Art Agency

MOLE RATS

David Curl/Oxford Scientific Films

ALL TEETH AND FEET

FEW ANIMALS COULD BE LESS APPEALING THAN THE MOLE RATS, BUT LOOKS MEAN LITTLE TO THESE CREATURES: THEY SPEND MOST OF THEIR FASCINATING LIVES BELOW GROUND, HIDDEN FROM OUR EYES

S mall mammals gain one big advantage from living underground—there is less chance of being caught by predators. Indeed, certain rodents have become so well adapted to a burrowing lifestyle that they look like moles—hence the term *mole rats*.

Names are deceiving, however; mole rats are not closely related to moles but are thought to be relatives of the cavies and porcupines, which together form the rodent suborder Hystricomorpha. The mole rats share certain anatomical features with the caviomorphs, but while most other members of this order are found in South America, mole rats are found in Africa and Eurasia. The gundis are another family of caviomorphs found in northern Africa.

There are two mole rat families: the African mole rats, or blesmols, family Bathyergidae; and the Eurasian, or blind, mole rats, family Spalacidae. The African mole rats comprise five genera in two subfamilies: the dune, common, Cape, silvery, and

The African mole rats and gundis are usually classified with the Caviomorpha suborder—the cavylike rodents—which contains 188 species within 18 families. The Eurasian, or blind, mole rats are allied to the Old World rats and mice in the subfamily Murinae.

ORDER
Rodentia
rodents

SUBORDER
Hystricomorpha

FAMILY
Bathyergidae

SUBFAMILY
Bathyerginae
Dune mole rats

SUBFAMILY
Georychinae
Common mole rats
Cape mole rat
Silvery mole rats
Naked mole rat

FAMILY
Spalacidae
Blind mole rats

FAMILY
Ctenodactylidae
Gundis

Rocky desert outcrops provide gundis with safe refuges and shade from the burning sun.

naked mole rats. In size, they all lie within a range of 4–13 in (10–33 cm) or so, but they vary in appearance and habits. The African mole rats typically have short-limbed, stocky bodies with thick, woolly or velvety fur. The one startling exception is the naked mole rat, which is almost entirely hairless.

AFRICAN TUNNELERS

An African mole rat is ideally formed for tunnel life. Its skin hangs loosely on its cylindrical body, which helps when negotiating tight corners. The large feet and hands have naked palms. The skull is large in order to support the two pairs of huge incisor teeth, the mole rat's main excavating tools. The lower incisors, in particular, often project sharply forward and can be moved independently. The mole rat avoids swallowing soil by folding a pair of hairy lips across its mouth behind its teeth.

African mole rats have tiny eyes; certainly near-sighted, they may actually be blind, using only the eyes' surface for detecting breezes in the burrow that indicate tunnel damage. The ears and nose, too, are specially modified. The nostrils can be closed, but the sense of smell is good. The external ears are mere disks of naked skin; but, like moles, mole rats are highly sensitive to sounds and vibrations. In many genera, too, there are touch-sensitive hairs all over the body.

HAIRLESS AND UNIQUE

Without doubt, the most bizarre member of this group is the naked mole rat, or sand puppy. Although many mole rats make interesting pets, naked mole

NAKED SURVIVORS

They may look helpless, but naked mole rats actually live longer than other mole rats. The reason for this may lie in a combination of factors. Because they live in relatively large colonies and feed on underground tubers, naked mole rats have been able to evolve an exclusively underground existence and thus become virtually invulnerable to predators. This in turn has allowed them to become almost blind and to lose the energy-consuming biological machinery needed to regulate body temperature. They also live longer as a result of lower predation, because lower mortality rates have been shown to slow down the aging process.

Kaj Halberg/Biofoto

African root rats (below) *are surprisingly similar in appearance and habit to the mole rats.*

Jane Burton/Bruce Coleman Ltd.

rats need precise conditions that few private individuals can provide. Wrinkled, bruise-colored, and virtually hairless, mole rats permanently resemble newborns. It is, however, not completely nude. A few pale, touch-sensitive hairs are scattered over its body, and its feet are fringed with fine hairs. These help when digging: The mole rat uses them to rake and sweep the soil behind it. In addition, there are whiskery, sensitive hairs on and around the lips.

The naked mole rat spends all of its life underground. Like its cousins, it has tiny eyes and ear flaps and seals off its nostrils when tunneling. Because its skin lacks both sweat glands and a fatty underlayer, its ability to regulate its body temperature is poorer than that of any other mammal. This, however, is hardly a problem under the ground.

Perhaps the oddest feature of the naked mole rat is its social behavior. It lives in large colonies, within which the hierarchy is more like that of bees or wasps than of other mammals. Only one pair breeds, and the remaining colony members belong to castes distinguished by their size and colonial duties. Mole rats are the only mammals in which this form of social structure, called eusocial, is known to exist.

THREE BLIND MOLE RATS

The three species of Eurasian mole rats have plump, round, rat-sized bodies. Their eyes are tiny, the size of poppy seeds, and lie under the skin. These are the only rodents in which the eyes have no function at all, hence their alternative name of blind mole rats. They have a line of stiff sensory hairs along each side of their thick, broad heads, and they have horny snouts.

DESERT COMBERS

Gundis, of which there are four genera and five species, look like chinchillas, their distant caviomorph relatives. They are mouse- to rat-sized with a short, furry tail. Unlike mole rats, gundis do not tunnel; their soft, silky fur, however, keeps them warm on cold desert nights. Their ear flaps are small, with hairs to keep out the sand. The skull is slim, and the ribs can be compressed inward; these features enable gundis to slip into rock crevices, where their long and bristly whiskers, or vibrissae, help them navigate. Their large eyes enable them to see when they move suddenly from bright daylight into the darkness of a crevice.

A gundi's toes have dense pads on the under-sides. These help it cling to rock surfaces, while at the same time shielding the feet from heat. The strong, pointed claws are useful for climbing rocks but unsuitable for grooming. As a result, the inner digits of a gundi's hind feet are equipped with comblike bristles, and these are used for grooming instead. ■

THE MOLE RATS' AND GUNDIS' FAMILY TREE

The mole rats and gundis are classified here with the suborder Hystricomorpha of cavylike rodents, although some authorities do not recognize the link— mainly because most of the cavylike rodents are found in South America. Their relationship to the cavies is based primarily upon the arrangement of their jaw muscles. Furthermore, some authorities place the Eurasian, or blind, mole rats with the Old World rats and mice, subfamily Murinae.

DUNE MOLE RAT
Bathyergus
(bah-thee-ER-gus)

The two species of dune mole rats are larger than other African mole rats **and dig mostly with their feet, which reduces their tunneling efficiency. However,** **they have specialized claws on all four feet to help them dig more effectively.**

SUBFAMILY
BATHYERGINAE

BLIND MOLE RATS
FAMILY SPALACIDAE

ⒶNCESTORS

BIRBALOMYS

The origins of mole rats can be traced back over 30 million years. Fossil remains of an animal known as *Gypsorhychus* (jip-so-RIE-kuss), similar in appearance to today's Cape mole rat, have been found in both Mongolia and Namibia.

The fossil history of the gundis goes back 50 million years to the Eocene epoch, when members of this family lived in Asia. The four living genera of gundis appear to have originated in Africa some 20 million years ago.

Birbalomys (bur-bah-LOE-miss) is considered to be the most primitive rodent, living some 50 million years ago in Asia. Very little is known about it, and the reconstruction shown below is highly speculative.

OLD WORLD
PORCUPINES

COMMON MOLE RAT

Cryptomys hottentotus
(*crip-TO-miss hot-en-TOT-uss*)

OTHER SPECIES:
SILVERY MOLE RATS
CAPE MOLE RATS

There are three species of common mole rats. Their fur varies in color from whitish through pale yellows and browns to almost black, and there is sometimes a white spot on the head. Like most of the African mole rats, they dig with their incisor teeth, which are reinforced by roots that extend behind the cheek teeth.

NAKED MOLE RAT

Heterocephalus glaber
(*het-eh-ro-KEF-al-uss GLAY-ber*)

By far the most bizarre in appearance of all the mole rats, the naked mole rat is found in arid regions of eastern Africa. A curious element of its lifestyle is its social structure, which is similar to that of bees and wasps.

SUBFAMILY
GEORYCHINAE

GUNDIS

Ctenodactylidae
(*ten-o-dak-TIL-ee-die*)

Gundis live in arid regions of northern Africa. The family name, meaning "comb-fingers," refers to the comblike grooming bristles on the insteps of their hind feet.

SPECIES:
SPEKE'S PECTINATOR
MZAB GUNDI
FELOU GUNDI
COMMON GUNDI
DESERT GUNDI

NEW WORLD
CAVYLIKE RODENTS

CAVYLIKE RODENTS

ANATOMY:
THE NAKED MOLE RAT

THE EYES

are tiny and almost useless. The mole rat usually closes its eyelids when their body is touched.

THE EARS

have no external pinnae (flaps), but they are otherwise normal and highly sensitive.

Dune mole rats (above left) are the largest of the African species, reaching 15 in (380 mm) from head to tail. The naked mole rat (above center) is much smaller (see Fact File box). Gundis (above right) are 6.3–9.5 in (160–240 mm) long from head to rump, with a 0.4–2 in (10–50 mm) tail.

THE NOSTRILS

can be sealed off to keep out sand while the mole rat digs. They retain, however, an excellent sense of smell.

THE INCISOR TEETH,

which grow constantly, are very long and project forward. The lower incisors are independently movable to aid digging.

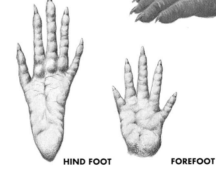

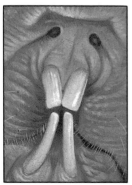

LIP GUARDS
A close-up of the mole rat's mouth reveals lips that close behind, rather than in front of, the incisors. The mole rat uses its twin incisor pairs as pickaxes to tunnel huge distances through soil and sand, and the lip barrier helps to keep the excavated debris out of the animal's mouth.

FEET
The forefeet (left) are short, since they are used very little in digging. The hind feet (far left) are markedly longer, being used to move soil.

HIND FOOT   FOREFOOT

Typical of its family, the naked mole rat has a compact, elongated skeleton with short limbs, reflecting its low, cylindrical form. In these respects, it is superficially similar to the American prairie dogs. The hind feet are long, and the mole rat uses these to paddle soil backward as it tunnels.

NAKED MOLE RAT SKELETON

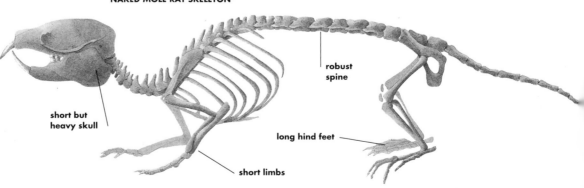

robust spine

short but heavy skull

long hind feet

short limbs

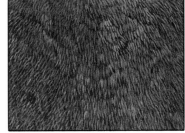

The naked mole rat's intricately wrinkled skin is scattered with a few fine hairs.

The common mole rat is more typical of its family in possessing thick, velvety fur.

CLASSIFICATION

GENUS: *HETEROCEPHALUS*
SPECIES: *GLABER*

SIZE

HEAD–BODY LENGTH: 3–3.5 IN (8–9 CM)
TAIL LENGTH: 1–1.5 IN (3–4 CM)
WEIGHT: 1–3 OZ (28–85 G)
WEIGHT AT BIRTH: 0.07 OZ (2 G)

COLORATION

BLUISH-PINK TO YELLOW SKIN
PALE YELLOW HAIRS

FEATURES

ALMOST NAKED SKIN
LARGE HANDS AND FEET
PROMINENT INCISOR TEETH
SENSITIVE VIBRISSAE AROUND MOUTH
VERY SMALL EYES
NO EXTERNAL EARS
NO SWEAT GLANDS
NO LAYER OF FAT BENEATH THE SKIN

THE SKIN
is loose, allowing the mole rat to move around a little inside it. The sparse hairs are touch-sensitive.

THE BODY
is low and barrel shaped to improve streamlining.

THE LEGS
are squat but powerful, although the naked mole rat uses them little in actual digging.

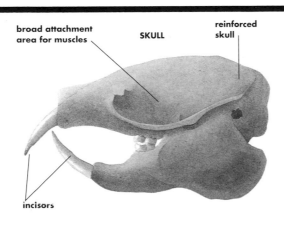

A mole rat possesses a typically short but solidly built skull, which is heavily reinforced in order to support the huge incisors. The eye sockets are much reduced, since the animal has little need for sharp vision. In fact, the eye sockets are largely occupied by the highly developed cheek muscles, which give immense power to the mole rat's jaw-closing mechanism.

broad attachment area for muscles

SKULL

reinforced skull

incisors

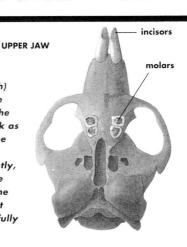

incisors

UPPER JAW

molars

The high-crowned molars (cheek teeth) are dwarfed by the massive incisors. The upper incisors work as a fixed pair, but the lower pair can be moved independently, since, in all but one mole rat species, the lower left and right jawbones are not fully fused at the front.

incisors

molars

FOR QUEEN AND COLONY

WITH THEIR SUPERBLY ADAPTED INCISORS AND BODY SHAPE, IT IS HARDLY SURPRISING THAT MOLE RATS REPRESENT SOME OF THE MOST ACCOMPLISHED BURROWERS IN THE WORLD OF MAMMALS

With one or two exceptions, mole rats are colonial animals, and the most supremely organized colonies are those of the eusocial naked mole rat. Studies of captive colonies of naked mole rats indicate that each colony consists of about 20–30 animals, although colonies of up to 100 individuals have been reported. A colony is led by a single, dominant female called the queen. Below the queen in the hierarchy is a small group of male nonworkers, but most of the rest are male and female workers. The workers are smaller than the dominant female and her nonworkers, but their size is not related to their age; many of them are younger than the nonworkers, but they are nevertheless fully adult.

Within the naked mole rat colony, the dominant female does all the breeding, and she and her group of nonworkers spend most of their time in the nesting chamber, emerging only to urinate or defecate. The remainder of the work—digging tunnels and finding food—is done by the workers. Activity, particularly burrowing, is generally restricted to early morning and late afternoon. In this way the workers avoid extreme temperatures near the surface. Most burrowing is done during the rainy season, when the soil is easiest to dig.

MINING MAYHEM

In any one habitat, it is normal to find just one genus of a family of strictly burrowing animals. African mole rats, however, are a notable exception to this rule: Common mole rats, Cape mole rats, and dune mole rats can be found living cheek by jowl in parts of the Cape province of South Africa. Actual contact between the different genera, which might well result in fights, is probably prevented by the fact that the tunnels are different sizes, but it is often difficult to distinguish between

the mounds of soil excavated by the different genera, and the ground may become so honeycombed with their tunnels that it becomes impossible to ride over it on horseback. Even a person walking may sink into the ground, and mole rats have been known to undermine railroad sleepers, with the result that the track subsides noticeably as trains pass.

Common mole rats live in small colonies of up to 25 individuals. Such a colony probably consists of an extended family comprising several generations. They share the whole burrow system and all sleep in the same nest. There appears to be some division of labor, with most of the work being done by the

George Crowther/Wilma George

Peter Johnson/NHPA

Mole rats (above) *fit snugly within their burrows, plugging unused entrances to deter predators.*

Gundis in the desert use the heating and cooling properties of rock to control their body temperatures.

smaller members. However, if they come across members of another colony they are extremely aggressive and may inflict savage bites.

Common mole rats communicate using a variety of squeaks, grunts, and growls. They may be active at any time of the day or night, but each animal has about five major rest periods in any 24-hour period. Most of the burrowing activity occurs during the wet seasons; new tunnels are dug to fresh feeding areas and food is carried back to the center of the system for storage. Common mole rats are rarely seen on the surface, but they do sometimes go above ground in order to gather nesting materials and dig up seeds.

Dune mole rats form small, close-knit colonies. Silvery mole rats and Cape mole rats, on the other hand, live alone. Although the burrow systems of individual Cape mole rats may come within a few feet or so of one another, they never interconnect. If

---

DUNE MOLE RATS ARE PRODIGIOUS DIGGERS, RESENTING ANY INTERRUPTION TO THEIR BURROWING ACTIVITIES

---

strange adults do come into contact, they fight, very often to the death. They are strictly burrowing animals and spend almost their entire lives underground. This is also the case with silvery mole rats, although these animals do appear to venture out sometimes, since their remains have been found in owl pellets.

The blind mole rats of Eurasia also live solitary lives. During any one 24-hour period, a blind mole rat may be active several times, but there appears to be no regular activity cycle.

DESERT COLONIES

Gundis live in colonies. The species known as Speke's pectinator, which is found in Ethiopia, forms colonies that occupy an area of 16,000–21,500 square feet (1,500–2,000 square meters). They are fairly common animals, but even when there are a number of gundis about, they are difficult to see, because their sandy-brown fur blends in perfectly with the rocks.

Individuals appear to warn others of danger with a long-drawn-out "whee, whee" call. The gundis of Morocco and Libya communicate with a birdlike whistle, and when alarmed they thump their hind feet on the ground. To escape from snakes and birds of prey, they scurry with great alacrity into rock fissures or piles of stones. ■

HABITATS

Mole rats are found in deserts, savannas, woodlands, and forests—anywhere, in fact, where the soil is suitably soft, although loose, sandy soils are the favorite. Mounds of excavated soil, which in some cases are very large, are a clear sign that mole rats are not far away.

Of all the African mole rats, the most extensively studied are the common mole rats, which are found through much of Africa, from Ghana eastward to Sudan and northern Uganda, and southward through Angola, Zaire, Zambia, Tanzania, and Malawi to Namibia and South Africa.

Common mole rats readily dig through a wide variety of soils, but the depth of the tunnel systems they create is directly related to soil consistency. Normally the burrow system lies 4–8 in (10–20 cm) below the surface, but the looser the soil, the greater the depth to which these animals dig. In some places, tunnels have been found as deep as 30 in (76 cm) below the surface.

THE BURROW SYSTEMS OF MOLE RATS ARE
PROBABLY THE LONGEST DUG AND
MAINTAINED NETWORKS OF ANY ANIMAL

Each burrow system contains a single communal sleeping nest, lined with vegetation and usually lying 6–8 in (15–20 cm) below the surface. There are several more round chambers, some or all of which are used for storing food. The main living areas and food stores are usually built on high ground, from which tunnels radiate in all directions. The total length of the burrow system can be anywhere from 165–1,115 ft (50–340 m), and it may cover an area of 4,740–64,600 sq ft (440–6,000 sq m).

African mole rats often burrow beneath termite mounds, which offer protection from heavy rains. In regions that flood seasonally, they may even tunnel up into a termite mound. Some colonies simply build their own large mound, inside which the burrow chambers are raised far enough above ground level to remain dry at all times.

BURROWING TECHNIQUES
With the exception of the Cape mole rat, mole rats dig with their teeth. Then, with cupped forefeet, they scrape the debris under their bodies, heaping it up behind them with the hind feet.

When a mole rat has built up a pile of soil as large as itself, it pushes it backward down the tunnel, using its hind feet and tail; bristly hairs on the feet and tail help to sweep the soil along if it is dry and finely crumbled. When the mole rat reaches an opening to the surface, it stands on its forefeet and expels the plug of soil. The resulting mounds may be 4–20 ft (1.2–6.1 m) apart.

The final stage of the operation consolidates the soil and prevents it from falling back down. For a second or two, the mole rat drums its hind feet against the soil plug to compress the particles into a brick. The feet vibrate at up to 24 vibrations a second. At first, the brick projects vertically from the center of the mole hill, but as it dries it crumbles and topples over, adding to the growing mound. The opening to the burrow, however, remains plugged.

Excavations take place mostly during the wet season, when the soil is easier to work. Any new food sources exposed by the process are left to be exploited at a later date. During the dry season, the mole rats work at lower levels and dispose of the soil they excavate in old tunnels.

The single species of silvery mole rat lives in eastern Africa, over an area that includes Kenya, Tanzania, Zaire, eastern Zambia, Malawi, and Mozambique. Its lifestyle is similar to that of common mole rats, and it digs its tunnels in much the same way. As it shifts the soil, it gives itself extra support by thrusting its nose and upper incisors into the top of the burrow.

The Cape mole rat occurs mostly in the southern and southwestern parts of Cape of Good Hope Province in South Africa, although there are also

J. A. Bailey/Ardea

Volcano-like mounds of soil, expelled during excavation, are characteristic of the naked mole rat. Unlike other mole rats, the entrances are not plugged closed.

Jane Burton/Bruce Coleman Ltd.

Sand can be easily worked by mole rats and provides an excellent burrowing medium.

small populations in Natal and southeastern Transvaal. The line of its underground burrow is clearly marked at the surface by a line of mounds. The main burrow leads into a round, smooth-walled chamber in which the animal stores food.

Of the two species of dune mole rats, one is found in the extreme southwestern part of Namibia and along the coast in northwestern South Africa. The other occurs farther south, along the coast of southern and southwestern South Africa. Dune mole rats, as their name implies, are found only in dunes and sandy flats. They are most common near coasts, but they also occur at elevations of up to 4,900 ft (1,490 m). They dig with their feet, rather than their teeth, and they push the excavated soil in front of them through the burrows, throwing it out through short side tunnels that lead to the surface. Dune mole rats shift a huge amount of soil: The Cape species may pile up 1,100 lb (500 kg) of soil in a month.

The naked mole rat is found in central and eastern Ethiopia, central Somalia, and Kenya. It

TEAMWORK

Teamwork pervades every element of a naked mole rat colony, and burrowing is no exception. The animal at the front of a digging party chisels away at the worked face with its teeth to loosen the soil. It then uses each forefoot alternately to paw at the soil, and finally scrapes with both forefeet at once to push the material behind it. A second mole rat collects this soil and starts to push it backward toward the opening, to the team member whose task it is to eject the soil from the burrow.

As the "pusher" mole rat moves, its place is taken by yet another individual, which in turn also collects a small pile of soil and begins the backward journey to the opening. At any one time, therefore, there are several mole rats scrabbling soil backward down the tunnel and several more moving forward, straddling the soil-pushers as they go. At intervals the digger and the ejector are relieved by other members of the team.

The burrow entrance remains open all the time, and there is a constant stream of soil being hurled out. As a result, the active burrow entrance often resembles an erupting volcano.

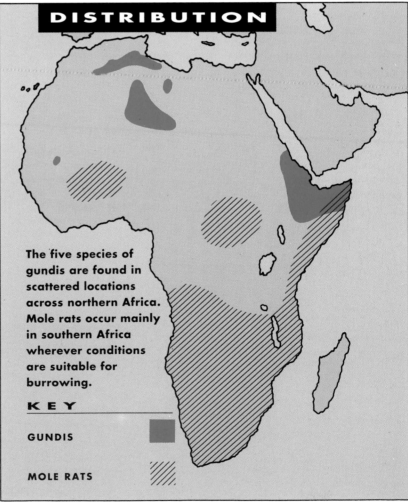

DISTRIBUTION

The five species of gundis are found in scattered locations across northern Africa. Mole rats occur mainly in southern Africa wherever conditions are suitable for burrowing.

KEY

GUNDIS

MOLE RATS

occurs in a variety of different types of soil, at elevations of 1,300–4,900 ft (400–1,500 m). It spends all its life underground and is only seen on the surface when forced there by a predator. A colony may have over 1,000 ft (300 m) of tunnels radiating out from a large, communal nesting chamber. Colonies are sometimes located very close to one another, with the result that the tunnel systems may appear to be much larger than they really are.

Blind mole rats occur in an area around the Mediterranean Sea that includes southeastern Europe to the Caspian Sea and the eastern parts of the extreme north of Africa. They live in steppe landscapes in a variety of soil and at a wide range of elevations. In Turkey, for example, they are found at heights of up to 8,300 ft (2,500 m). They dig with their incisors and bulldoze the soil out through openings with their heads. The tunnel system lies deep, up to 12 ft (3.7 m) below the surface in places, especially in winter. Here the sleeping and food-storage chambers are located, together with a sanitary chamber, which is walled up when full. The feeding tunnels, which must have access to the roots and tubers of plants, are near the surface. Where blind mole rats live in places liable to flooding, they build large nesting mounds, sometimes 9 ft (2.7 m) in diameter and over 3 ft (1 m) high.

George Crowther/Wilma George

FOCUS ON

THE ETHIOPIAN HIGHLANDS

Some 40 million years ago, volcanic lava erupted over Ethiopia to produce massive highland ranges. When land later subsided to create the monumental Great Rift Valley, the Ethiopian highlands were split into two regions. Surrounded by arid plains, these highlands were effectively isolated islands, and through the course of evolution their native wildlife has developed unique adaptations to this specialized environment.

The Balé Mountains, in the center of Ethiopia, are home not only to Speke's gundi but also to mole rats, whose constant burrowing over thousands of years has considerably altered the terrain. These rodents must take their chances with the numerous predators, such as the simien jackal. Naked mole rats establish their colonies on the lower slopes and desert plains.

TEMPERATURE AND RAINFALL

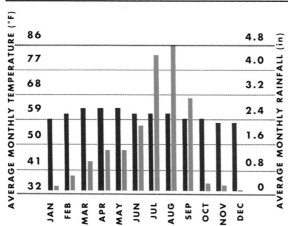

■ **TEMPERATURE**

■ **RAINFALL**

Ethiopia's highlands experience a tropical climate altered by the high altitudes. Temperatures are fairly consistent on average, although the nights can be very cold. Heavy monsoon rains fall in July and August.

The gundis are all found in northern Africa, in desert or semidesert habitats, at any elevation from sea level to 7,800 ft (2,400 m). They never create or even use burrows, not even for nests. Instead, they use caves and rock crevices as temporary shelters. Areas with rocky cliffs and ledges for sunbathing make ideal habitats for gundis. They move rapidly with their bellies almost touching the ground. They are excellent climbers and, using their sharp claws aided by the comblike bristles on their feet, can scale almost vertical rockfaces. ■

NEIGHBORS

Ethiopia contains vast tracts of remote, hilly terrain. It is a haven for several endemic species of plants and animals. The valleys come alive during the wet season, attracting grazing mammals.

CRESTED PORCUPINE

A distant relative of the mole rats, this porcupine is an expert burrower. It feeds on roots and bulbs.

GERBIL

The gerbils are true desert specialists, hopping rapidly over the soft sand on their long hind limbs.

Illustrations Joanne Cowne

Cut in two by the east Great Rift Valley, the highlands cover almost half of Ethiopia's entire area. Bordering the Red Sea to the east, the mountains sweep to a maximum altitude of 14,760 ft (4,500 m) in the north of the country.

HIGHLANDS

RED SEA

SAUDI ARABIA

ETHIOPIA

AFRICAN BARN OWL
The gundi can hear the rustle of wings as a barn owl swoops—but it does not always escape its clutches.

SAW-SCALED ADDER
This African viper can slip effortlessly over the rocky outcrops where gundis make their homes.

AFRICAN GOSHAWK
Goshawks pounce on their prey either from fast, low-level flight or from a great height.

MODERATELY DANGEROUS

MODERATELY DANGEROUS

MODERATELY DANGEROUS

LEOPARD

The leopard's widespread distribution owes a great deal to its ability to exploit small prey.

AFRICAN WILD DOG

These hunting dogs are superbly skilled predators, relying on close teamwork to chase and tackle prey.

JERBOA

With hind limbs four times the length of its forelegs, a jerboa packs a powerful kick when jumping.

CHEETAH

Africa's champion sprinter, the cheetah is equipped to chase down its prey at lightning speed.

SIMIEN JACKAL

Jackals form long-lasting pair bonds, relying on the partnership for successful hunting and pup rearing.

FOOD AND FEEDING

Mole rats feed almost exclusively on the underground parts of plants. As a result, they are regarded as pests in some agricultural areas, but they may also be of some benefit in that they eat plants that are poisonous to domestic animals.

When feeding on small items, the mole rat usually holds the food in its forefeet. It shakes off the soil, cuts the food up with its incisors, and chews it with its cheek teeth. Mole rats do not need to drink; they lose very little water in their damp underground habitat and their food has a high moisture content.

LARDERS FULL OF ROOTS

Common mole rats sometimes venture above ground, where they may collect aloe leaves and seeds. Occasionally they eat invertebrate animals, such as earthworms, cockchafer larvae, and white ants. However, most of the diet consists of bulbs, tubers, and rhizomes.

The Cape mole rat stores its food in a single large chamber. It is said to bite off the buds of bulbs and tubers to stop them from sprouting, thus ensuring that the stored nutrients are not used up in producing new shoots and stems—a practice that, obviously, does little to endear the species to tuber-crop farmers.

Unlike other mole rats, the dune mole rat's grooved teeth (below) *are rarely used for digging.*

John Visser/Bruce Coleman Ltd.

Dune mole rats, too, store their food in their burrows. They feed mainly on roots and tubers, but because of their large size and poorer digging ability, they cannot afford to be too choosy and therefore eat a range of grasses and herbs as well. In agricultural areas they often collect an enormous surplus of food; they are particularly partial to potatoes.

While the silvery mole rat feeds on bulbs and tubers and is said to damage potato crops in some areas, it does not appear to hoard. Instead, food is always left where it is, thus ensuring that it continues to grow. In this way the animal provides itself with a food supply that constantly replenishes itself. Naked mole rats also leave their food in place—in any case, the huge tubers that grow where naked mole rats are found can weigh up to 110 lb (50 kg) and are often too large to move. Individual mole rats visit the growing roots and tubers whenever they need to, with the result that a large tuber gradually becomes hollowed out.

Blind mole rats feed on a wider range of plant materials that includes not only roots, tubers, and rhizomes but also stalks, leaves, and fruits. They

NO GNAWING

Gundis sit on rocky outcrops nibbling flowers, leaves, and grasses—a diet that takes into account the fact that these little animals lack the hardened teeth typical of many rodents.

CUPBOARD

Common mole rats collect food that is small and easy to move and store it in underground chambers. Their diet typically includes tubers, bulbs, and roots.

insight

NOT A DROP!

Gundis do not drink; they seem to get all their water from the plants they eat. Even the Mzab gundi, which lives in the plains and mountains just north of the Sahara, never has a drop. It lacks any major physiological adaptations for conserving its water—other than moderate urine concentration—or for controlling its body temperature, despite the harsh conditions in which it lives. Instead, it relies on the shade afforded by the rocks and the high water content of succulent desert plants on which it feeds (see Survival, page 1376).

store what they cannot eat at the time—parts from up to thirteen different species of plants have been found in the storage chambers of some blind mole rats. One researcher found 77 lb (35 kg) of potatoes in one storage chamber!

FORAGING FAR AND WIDE

Gundis feed above ground. They eat leaves, stalks, seeds, and flowers, but they are not known to eat any animal material. The moisture content in the plant matter provides their water needs. Their teeth do not have the hard orange enamel typical of so many other rodents, so gundis do not gnaw very much. Since food is scarce in the dry regions in which they live, gundis often have to forage over a wide area; a gundi may travel up to 0.6 mi (1 km) each morning. Gundis do not store food, nor do they at any time build up a store of fat in their bodies. ∎

Wendy Bramall/Wildlife Art Agency

1369

SOCIAL STRUCTURE

Mole rats are aggressive. In species that live solitary lives, individuals often fight if they meet, and even in colonial species tolerance of others is limited to members of the same colony. But this is not unusual. What is unique is the tendency toward eusocial behavior shown by some species, and taken to its extreme by the naked mole rat.

A RECENT DISCOVERY

Eusocial behavior is common among certain ants, wasps, and bees, but until recently it was unknown among mammals. The eusocial lifestyle of the naked mole rat was discovered during the 1970s. Richard Alexander, an American biologist, had already offered the inspired prediction that, somewhere, there could be a social mammal with a caste system just like that of a colony of wasps, in which nonreproductive workers helped one or more reproductive individuals to raise their young.

A lunar landscape of volcanoes (right) *marks the site of an extensive naked mole rat colony.*

F. Hartmann/Frank Lane Picture Agency

The idea was taken up by an ecophysiologist, Jenny Jarvis, working in Cape Town, who had spent several years studying naked mole rats. She had noticed how naked mole rats cooperated with one another and realized that what she already knew about them fitted well with Alexander's idea. She therefore decided to take another look at the species and in 1981 announced her conclusion that the naked mole rat is indeed eusocial, with each colony being dominated by a single reproductive female, or queen.

SELF-CONTAINED COLONIES

A colony of naked mole rats is self-contained, which means that it contains a number of closely related animals, many with the same parents. Such close relationships are thought to have been an important factor in the evolution of eusocial behavior. The queen does all the breeding, with two breeding males, and she suckles her offspring. But the young are otherwise raised by the nonbreeding workers.

Researchers believe that the queen produces a chemical, probably a pheromone, that suppresses the breeding abilities of the other females. She makes regular patrols along the tunnels, pushing the workers out of the way as she goes, and it is

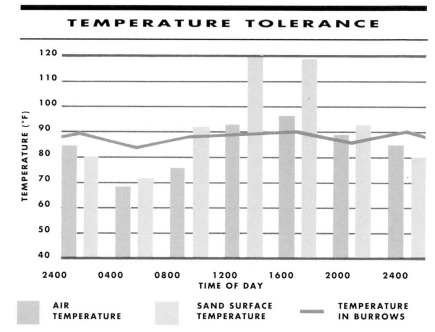

TEMPERATURE TOLERANCE

Legend:
- AIR TEMPERATURE
- SAND SURFACE TEMPERATURE
- TEMPERATURE IN BURROWS

A burrowing lifestyle enables desert-living mole rats to escape the worst of the temperature extremes. Sand is an efficient absorber of the sun's heat, and by the early afternoon its surface is burning hot—far hotter than the air around it. At the depths inhabited by the mole rats, however, the sand is comfortably tolerable.

probably this physical aggression, combined with the effect of the pheromone, that ensures that a worker will not breed. Near the nest chamber is a communal latrine area, and it may be that chemicals in the queen's urine affect the workers as they visit the area. The ovaries of a nonbreeding female are very poorly developed, but if the queen dies, one of the nonbreeding females develops rapidly and takes her place.

Eusocial behavior also exists to a lesser extent among common mole rats. Here, too, the colony appears to be dominated by one large, breeding female, but in most cases the workers pay less attention to her offspring and there is no difference between male breeders and nonbreeders.

In one species, however—the Damaraland mole rat—the social structure is similar to that of the naked mole rat: The workers spend much of their time taking care of the pups, preventing them from straying, grooming them, keeping them warm, and feeding them after they have been weaned. But if the queen dies she is not replaced, because there seems to be some process that prevents breeding between the closely related members of the rest of the colony. Exactly what it is that suppresses their reproductive instincts is not yet understood, but it must be something to do with the specific chemistry of the colony, because if a nonbreeding male and female from different colonies are put together, they begin courting almost immediately.

Naked mole rats and common mole rats are the only known eusocial mammals. In a dune mole rat colony, all the females breed and all the other mole rats live solitary lives. Eusocial behavior yields a

DOWN UNDER

A typical burrow system (left) *includes food supplies and a main chamber for the breeding female, her offspring, and the nonworkers. Digging teams* (foreground and top right of picture) *work together to extend the network of tunnels.*

RAT RACE

Naked mole rats differ in size from the large queen (top right), *through nonworking adults* (center right), *to the small adult workers* (below right).

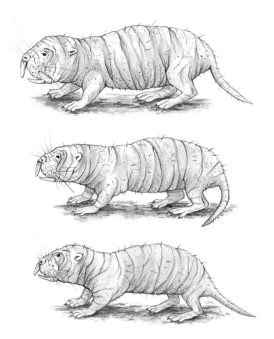

Illustrations Angela Hargreaves/Wildlife Art Agency

Nonbreeding naked mole rats spend around 60 percent of their time resting in the nest.

number of advantages. A solitary mole rat, or even a pair, living in an area where tubers are thinly distributed, would be hard put to find enough to eat without using up a lot of energy—energy needed for breeding and rearing, for example. In a colony, however, foragers are always at hand to stock the larders. Furthermore, small animals burrow much more quickly, and with less expenditure of energy, than large animals. The small naked mole rat workers, for example, are best employed in a burrowing role, while the large queen benefits by reserving her energies for reproduction.

GUNDI FAMILY LIFE

Gundis form colonies, within which the males and females occupy family territories with their young. When they forage, gundis travel singly or in small parties, but foraging takes place only at certain times of the day, because these animals spend much of their time exploiting sun and shade to regulate their body temperature.

David Curl/Oxford Scientific Films

The gundi becomes active after sunrise, when it emerges from its den to feed. Over the next few hours it alternately feeds and takes long sunbaths to warm up its body. It sunbathes by spreading itself out flat against a rock, with its hind feet splayed, to collect as much heat as possible.

After about 10:30 A.M., however, the desert starts to heat up and the gundi's activity decreases. It spends most of the rest of the day in the shade, becoming active again at about 5:00 P.M. Its fur protects it from much of the desert heat, and therefore much time is spent grooming in order to keep the fur in good condition.

Gundis need warmth to keep their bodies working. On cold and windy days they may not venture out at all. Rain is dangerous for them because their soft fur is not designed to keep water out.

PLAYING POSSUM

Gundis make no attempt to bite, even in self-defense; instead, they feign death. Frightened, they remain completely motionless. They may lie like this for a few seconds to a few hours, depending on how nervous they are. In one instance, a captive, fully tame gundi lay prone for twelve hours after being placed in a new cage. The expression "playing possum," applied to such behavior, derives from the Virginia opossum's habit of playing dead when unnerved. ■

Illustrations Kim Thompson

TAKE COVER!
Gundis are highly vocal. On detecting a predator, they warn the rest of the colony with loud squeaks (above), then bolts into a secure rock crevice.

PILEUPS
At night and when the weather is cold, gundis pile on top of one another to keep warm. Young are shielded from the crush by their mothers or lie buried in the fur at the back of their necks.

BODY HEAT

All mammal species can regulate their own body temperature by physiological means— all, that is, except naked mole rats. For these mole rats, however, temperature control is not a problem. They manage with a fairly low body temperature of 90°F (32°C), which is approximately the upper temperature limit found within the burrows. In fact, relying on ambient temperatures means that these animals avoid wasting precious energy reserves on keeping warm.

However, when the burrow temperature drops a couple of degrees, naked mole rats will often shiver rapidly to warm up. They also crouch down and nestle alongside other colony members in the resting chamber, benefiting from the collective, cozy body heat.

REPRODUCTION

In an established colony of naked mole rats, only one female produces offspring. However, before the colony's social hierarchy is fully established, any female may come into estrus, and those that do often fight to the death. Once the dominance of one female is established, however, the ability to breed is suppressed in all the others.

The dominant female initiates courtship, and her mate is usually a nonworking male. Breeding is timed so that most births occur during February, March, and April. This is the wettest part of the year, when food is most plentiful. If the first litter survives, the female does not breed again until the following year, but if anything happens to her offspring, she mates again; one female was observed to produce three litters in six months.

SLOW TO GROW

Litters contain three to twenty young, which are blind and, of course, naked. They are tended by workers, who keep them warm in the breeding chamber and move them to safety if danger threatens. The young mature very slowly. Their eyes open only after several weeks, and they do not reach adult size for at least a year. However, they start their lives as workers as soon as they are fully weaned, when they are one or two months old.

Reproduction among common mole rats is broadly similar, but breeding does not appear to be seasonal. The gestation period is marginally longer and no female produces more than two litters a year. The young are active within hours of birth and can defend themselves ably with their sharp incisors. Within twenty-four hours they start to wander out of the nest, and they are weaned at three weeks.

The silvery mole rat produces one litter of two or three young each year during the rainy season. Adults may live for up to three years. The Cape mole rat breeds between August and December, although courtship starts in June when males drum the ground with their hind feet to attract females. Females produce two litters each year, and since they are receptive again soon after giving birth to the first litter, they are pregnant again within ten days. Gestation lasts forty-four days and each litter may contain three to ten young. Within nine days, however, the young are fully furred and their eyes are open.

RATS' NEST

The naked mole rat queen suckles her young on a cozy bed of dried grasses in the nesting chamber (below). *When they are weaned, responsibility for their daily care is assumed by the nonbreeding adults.*

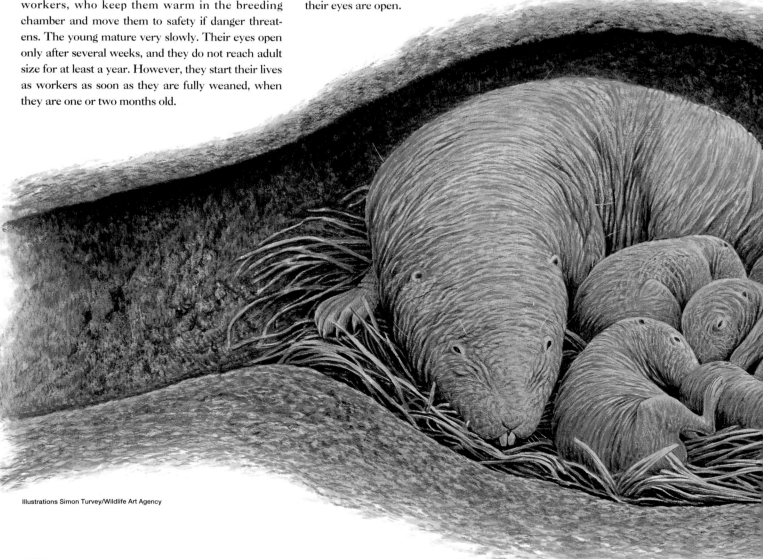

Illustrations Simon Turvey/Wildlife Art Agency

ROCK SINGERS

Gundi babies (above) *chirp constantly in their nest among the rocks; this helps the mother find them in a hurry. The rocky lair stays cool by day but retains heat at night.*

FROM BIRTH TO DEATH

NAKED MOLE RAT

GESTATION: 70 DAYS	**EYES OPEN:** SEVERAL WEEKS
LITTER SIZE: 3–20	**WEANING:** 1–2 MONTHS
BREEDING: NOVEMBER–JANUARY	**MATURITY:** OVER A YEAR
WEIGHT AT BIRTH: 0.07 oz (2 G)	**LONGEVITY:** 5 YEARS IN CAPTIVITY

COMMON MOLE RAT

GESTATION: 78–92 DAYS	**MOBILE:** WITHIN 24 HOURS
LITTER SIZE: 2–3	**WEANING:** 3 WEEKS
BREEDING: ASEASONAL; MAY OCCUR AT ANY TIME OF YEAR	**MATURITY:** NOT KNOWN
WEIGHT AT BIRTH: NOT KNOWN	**LONGEVITY:** OVER 2 YEARS IN CAPTIVITY

DESERT GUNDI

GESTATION: 56 DAYS	**EYES OPEN:** AT BIRTH
LITTER SIZE: 2	**WEANING:** 3–6 WEEKS
BREEDING: AT ANY TIME OF YEAR	**MATURITY:** 8–12 MONTHS
WEIGHT AT BIRTH: 0.6–1.4 oz (17–40 G)	**LONGEVITY:** 5 YEARS IN CAPTIVITY

Female dune mole rats probably come into season only once each year, and mating takes place toward the end of the winter rains in July and August. There are up to four young in the litter. The birth of the young appears to be timed so that they are weaned and start to dig their own burrows in the spring, when the soil is easiest to work.

The blind mole rats of Eurasia also produce one litter each year. Mating usually occurs from January to early March, but may run into April. Gestation takes about four weeks, after which two to four naked young are born. Although they weigh no more than 0.3 oz (8.5 g) at birth, they may reach independence at just two months old.

Gundis are born, after a gestation period of approximately fifty-six days, fully furred and with their

Gundis huddle on a warm rock (right), *soaking up the morning sunshine.*

eyes open; litters contain no more than one or two, occasionally three, offspring. They are born in a temporary den among the rocks, and if danger threatens, the mother carries her young to safety, holding them in her teeth by the skin on their necks, while another adult keeps a lookout from a point near the former den. Tucked into their place of refuge, the youngsters keep up a constant chirping.

A female gundi's nipples are located in unusual parts of the body; two are on the flanks, just behind the shoulder, and two are high on her chest just below the base of the neck. However, she produces little milk in the dry desert conditions; fortunately the young need relatively little nursing. She begins to wean them on chewed leaves at an early stage, and they are fully weaned after about four weeks. ∎

Kaj Halberg/Biofoto

DEFYING THE DESERTS

THESE RODENTS HAVE LITTLE TO FEAR FROM HUMANS; THE LAND ITSELF IS FAR MORE HOSTILE. LIFE AS A GUNDI INVOLVES A DAILY ROUND OF SUNBATHING AND SHELTERING, SIMPLY IN ORDER TO STAY ALIVE

On the whole, mole rats are not persecuted and most species are not thought to be endangered, although little is actually known about their current status. The only species of mole rat that is considered to be rare is *Bathyergus janetta*, one of the two species of dune mole rats. Its dune habitat is relatively limited, and parts of it are slowly disappearing as a result of diamond mining.

The only predators known to pursue naked mole rats underground are snakes. There is evidence that the mole snake and the eastern beaked snake are both attracted to the smell of freshly dug soil. Since the naked mole rat entrances are left open, snakes have little trouble getting inside. Other predators, such as carnivores and owls, only get the opportunity to pick off naked mole rats if they are working very close to the surface or they venture out of their burrows.

Gundis have been described as the most numerous mammals in North Africa. Local Arab people hunt them for food, particularly in Tunisia, where the species *Gundi gundi* grows plump on the relatively abundant food available. Occasionally, nomads passing a rocky desert outcrop will pause to capture a gundi, but these agile little mammals bolt remarkably quickly into their lairs. By and large, however, these animals are left alone by humans; they are harmless and do not compete for resources. They do, however, have a number of enemies in the rest of the animal kingdom, and gundis fall prey to snakes and birds. Wild mammal predators include jackals, but the largest numbers fall prey to domestic cats and dogs.

SURVIVORS OF THE SANDS
Despite this, the breeding capacity of these animals is quite sufficient to maintain numbers and, at present, conservation measures are not thought to be necessary. The gundis' very success seems to stem from their ability to thrive in areas where few humans can survive. A pressing question may then be how such a tiny mammal survives in one of the most inhospitable environments known to man.

Like many rodents adapted to arid lands, gundis have specialized kidneys, which recycle bodily fluids and concentrate urine. In the central Sahara, however, air temperatures can soar above 104°F (40°C). In such heat, the sand may reach a blazing 147°F (64°C). This can threaten the survival of a small mammal, even one as heat-tolerant as the

Gundis (above) *manage to survive in the desert by extracting precious moisture from plant matter.*

George Crowther/Wilma George

Richard Packwood/Oxford Scientific Films

This map shows existing deserts and areas under threat of desertification in Africa and the Middle East.

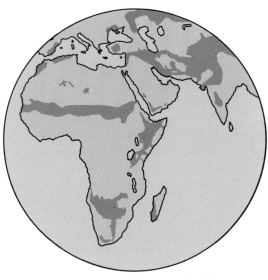

AREAS UNDER THREAT   EXISTING DESERTS

Northern Africa and the Middle East are dominated by the huge Sahara and Arabian Desert—and these deserts are expanding. Droughts, overgrazing, and overcropping are causing desertification south of the Sahara, in the Horn of Africa (Ethiopia and Somalia), and in southern Africa. In Africa alone, desertification affects the lives of over 100 million people, as well as countless animal species.

gundi. The desert gundi, *Ctenodactylus vali*, is perhaps the toughest of the family: It can excrete urine up to five times its normal concentration and can survive several hours in the highest temperatures.

CLINGING TO LIFE

The gundi perhaps least well adapted to desert life is the Mzab gundi. It lives in the Mzab region of central Algeria, where the Hoggar mountains rise to great heights. On the central plateaus, far from the humid winds blowing off the Mediterranean, rain may not fall for many years. It seems extraordinary that plants can survive far from the nearest coast. But water is ever present beneath the sands, draining from the heights toward the coast and condensing in the most unlikely sites—tiny outcrops of

A select few plants and animals are adapted to survive in the hostile desert environment.

rock in the middle of nowhere. The scant moisture feeds the wind-blown seeds—some of them hundreds of years old—and drought-resistant grasses or shrubs struggle into life.

The Mzab gundi fares reasonably well in the mountains, which are relatively cool and wet—rainfall may reach an annual 4 in (100 mm)—but in the central plateaus, conditions are barely tolerable. The gundi has only a limited ability to concentrate urine, and requires plant food with a mimimum 50 percent water content, particularly in the case of a lactating mother. How, then, does it survive?

One reason must be the presence, in certain areas, of succulent plants. But much of its success stems from its behavior. Sand is a hostile living

OUT OF ACTION

Mole rats are taken by snakes, especially during the rainy season when the soil is soft and penetrable. Isolated colonies also suffer when food is scarce; naked mole rats rely on high colony numbers in order to find enough food, and if too many mole rats die, the entire colony may starve.

A contagious disease, too, can be a killer: A single sick animal can quickly infect the entire colony, owing to the close-knit social structure.

ALONGSIDE MAN

UNLOVED BUT UNTROUBLED

Mole rats are not popular animals. They have little aesthetic appeal, and their activities can wreak havoc on agricultural crops and may damage property; they have been known to chew into buried cables. Their tunneling can cause railroad tracks and roads to subside, and their mounds may damage harvesting machines, devastate golf courses, and ruin suburban lawns. They appear, however, to be quite numerous and, being underground animals, they have relatively few enemies. In some places they are killed as pests, and some species are hunted for food by local people, but as yet human predation does not seem to have adversely affected their populations.

environment, but rocks heat up and cool down more slowly. As the sun rises, the air is still fairly cool and the gundi can scuttle comfortably over the rocks while it forages and, later, digests its meals. Seeking the juiciest plants, it eats up every scrap and wastes nothing. When cooling winds blow, the gundi finds a shady pocket of rock and stretches its body flat. At this point, heat convects and radiates rapidly from its spread eagled body to cool it down.

In such a way, the Mzab gundi's daily lifestyle helps it survive. But there is little doubt that, in the burning plateaus of Algeria, the Mzab gundi is clinging to a precarious existence, and it was probably much more common and widespread in former centuries when these regions were more humid. ■

Mole rats face few threats in the wild, being numerous and secure against most enemies. **Bathyergus janetta (below),** *of Namibia and South Africa, is believed to be the only species under threat.*

John Visser/Bruce Coleman Ltd.

INTO THE FUTURE

In the short term, there seems to be little danger that any of the mole rats or gundis, with the possible exception of the Namibian species of dune mole rat, will become extinct. Their activities are not, as yet, regarded as being sufficiently damaging to crops and property to warrant sustained extermination campaigns, and their habitats are not unduly threatened. It is possible to envisage a scenario in which the needs of African agriculture might reach a stage at which farmers would consider it necessary to wage war on the mole rats. If this were to become the case, it seems likely that their numbers would be rapidly reduced and some species might well be wiped out. For the time being, however, the survival of mole rats is not a problem, and general habitat protection is a good conservation measure.

Gundis as a whole are present in large numbers, and their rocky habitats have no commercial value

PREDICTION

SAFE IN THE BURROW

The mole rats' habit of plugging their extensive burrow systems renders them almost impregnable to the adverse effects of unfavorable climate and predation, and the group as a whole is safe for the foreseeable future.

or use. Their worst enemies, for the most part, have always been natural predators. One possible exception is the Felou gundi, whose range includes the drought-afflicted Sahel region of west Africa (see The Creeping Sands, right). The hardy Felou gundi will perhaps be one of the Sahel's longer-term residents, making do with whatever plant matter remains in the wake of the creeping sands. The changes to its ecosystem may ultimately prove too much for the gundi—but in a harsh region such as the Sahara, the human population is naturally more concerned for its own survival than that of a species of small rodent.

For the gundis as a whole, however, the natural swings of climate from hostile to favorable and the presence of wild predators are as important in their long-term survival as the environmental effects wrought by humans on their habitat. ∎

THE CREEPING SANDS

Established as a desert some five million years ago, the Sahara has experienced several swings between drought and humidity ever since, and its plants and animals have burgeoned or declined accordingly. In recent decades, however, an unprecedented environmental disaster has struck at the once-fertile Sahel region in the southern Sahara: desertification through soil erosion.

The Sahel is a zone of dry grassland stretching east to west across the southern Sahara border. The natural pastures, watered by the flooding Niger and Senegal Rivers, are vital grazing lands for the livestock of local people and an important stopover site for countless migratory bird species. There, too, lives the Felou gundi.

In the 1950s, the rainfall in the Sahel was higher than usual and the area of grazing land expanded. Farming people from the densely populated savanna moved into the Sahel. Their animals began to overgraze the land, while the people cut down trees and shrubs to use as firewood—the primary source of heat fuel in developing lands.

A series of droughts in the 1970s prevented the Sahel's plants from reestablishing themselves. Strong winds blew the bare soil away. Livestock died and, by 1973, an estimated 100,000 people had died from starvation or disease. Drought and famine struck again in 1983–1985, and the erosion extended southward into the savanna, then into the Sahara; the former grassland eventually turned into desert. Desertification would probably not have occurred had the land not been overgrazed before the onset of the droughts.

Illustration Evi Antoniou

INDEX

Published by Marshall Cavendish Corporation
99 White Plains Road
Tarrytown, New York 10591-9001

© Marshall Cavendish Corporation, 1997
© Marshall Cavendish Ltd, 1994

The material in this series was first published in the English language by Marshall Cavendish Limited, of 119 Wardour Street, London W1V 3TD, England.

Library of Congress Cataloging-in-Publication Data

Encyclopedia of mammals.
  p. cm.
  Includes index.
  ISBN 0-7614-0575-5 (set)   ISBN 0-7614-0584-4 (v. 9)

  Summary: Detailed articles cover the history, anatomy, feeding habits, social structure, reproduction, territory,
    and current status of ninety-five mammals around the world.
  1. Mammals—Encyclopedias, Juvenile. [1. Mammals—Encyclopedias.] I. Marshall Cavendish Corporation.
QL706.2.E54 1996
599'.003—dc20   96-17736
                                                          CIP
                                                          AC

Printed in Malaysia
Bound in U.S.A.